Love
TO LOVE
You

Love to Love You

Copyright © 1997 by Bill and Pam Farrel
Published by Harvest House Publishers
Eugene, Oregon 97402

For more information regarding Bill and Pam Farrel's resources,
newsletter, books, tapes, and speaking engagements, please send
a self-addressed, stamped envelope to:

    Masterful Living
    629 S. Rancho Santa Fe, #306
    San Marcos, CA 92069

Library of Congress Cataloging-in-Publication Data
Farrel, Bill, 1959-
        Love to love you / Bill and Pam Farrel.
          p. cm.
        ISBN 1-56507-686-9
        1. Man-woman relationships. 2. Interpersonal communication.
3. Love. 4. Intimacy (Psychology) I. Farrel, Pam, 1959-   . II. Title.
HQ801.F35 1997
306.7—dc21   97-9435
                                             CIP

Scripture verses are taken from: The Holy Bible, New International Version®, Copyright © 1973, 1978,
1984 by the International Bible Society. Used by permission of Zondervan Publishing House; and the
Living Bible, Copyright © 1971 owned by assignment by Illinois Regional Bank N.A. (as trustee).
Used by permission of Tyndale House Publishers, Inc., Wheaton, Illinois 60189. All rights reserved.

Design and production by Koechel Peterson & Associates, Minneapolis, Minnesota

Printed in the United States of America.

97 98 99 00 01 02 03 04 05 06 / DC / 10 9 8 7 6 5 4 3 2 1

To Jim and Sally

You have modeled real love

and given us your time, talent, and TLC.

We love you.

Contents

My heart was racing. The closer I got to home, the more excited I got. I'd been away from him for days. All I wanted was to feel his strong arms around me, to feel his lips on mine. I wanted to be all his, and I knew he wanted to be all mine. I thought, We've both felt this way before—many times. But that night, as I raced toward the one I love, my thoughts went back to the first time my heart raced at the thought of being in his presence.

I was dating Bill. I knew I loved him. I knew he was "the one," and I was driving two hours to meet him for dinner. Each mile I was hoping he felt the same way. Since that time, many days of anticipating being together have followed. Many days of enjoying each other heart to heart. Romantic connections—we all long for them.

As I turned the corner, my heart felt like it would come out of my chest with longing. This night was no different. Seventeen years later I still felt the same anticipation. Anticipation. This book is dedicated to helping you feel that joy and anticipation of being together and having your times together be as terrific as possible. May you often hear each other whisper "Love to love you!"

Love is a desire of the whole being
to be united to some other being.

SAMUEL TAYLOR COLERIDGE

C H A P T E R   1

Kiss of Hearts

ENCOURAGE YOUR LOVE WITH WORD AND DEED

Say only what is good and helpful . . .
and what will give . . . a blessing.

THE BOOK OF EPHESIANS

JENNY WAS EXCITED TO BE SO CLOSE TO THE BEACH. She had packed up the boys and headed out for the weekend campout. Blaine, her husband, was following in his car just a few minutes behind her. As Jenny crested the hill, the bright sunset blinded her for a moment. She hit the brakes, but it was too late. The sound of steel hitting steel broke her serene mood. She had accidentally run a red light. She checked to see that the boys were all right, then stepped from the car and was relieved to see that the people in the other car were all right as well. Suddenly she began to cry. Sirens, horns, loud voices— everything around her began to swirl. Then she felt it. Strong arms around her shoulders. Blaine gently pulled her face to his chest and all the confusion seemed to evaporate.

"Jenny, are you okay?"

She managed an affirmative nod.

"It'll be all right. It's just a car. It's not you or one of the kids or anyone else—just a car."

Together the two of them managed to exchange information with the other driver and police officers. Then, as they headed back to Blaine's car, a fireman who had been on the scene walked over to Blaine.

"Sir, I just want to thank you for doing it right. I see a lot of accidents, and I see a lot of angry husbands. But you, you did it right."

Jenny smiled and gave Blaine a hug.

The power of encouragement. Encouraging words, encouraging actions, encouraging gifts all fit together to create an atmosphere where love can blossom and flourish. Encouragement from the one you love most can mean more than life itself at times.

*Be kind and
compassionate to one another,
forgiving each other . . .*

THE BOOK OF EPHESIANS

❀ ENCOURAGING WORDS ❀

Bill unexpectedly came running into the house on one of those extra busy days, in one of those extra busy weeks. He stopped me, gave me a big squeeze and a kiss, then said, "Oh, I wish I was independently wealthy and could love you all day long." Then he left.

Over the next few days we had little time together, and, when Bill finally got a day off, he noticed that I kept following him around. I found plenty of reasons to touch him as I flirted with him, showing my love in small ways. He said, "Pam, what's up? Don't get me wrong. I love all this attention, but I haven't hardly been around all week. What's got you so interested in me?"

"You wished you were independently wealthy and could love me all day long."

The power of encouraging words!

I sometimes find myself getting so focused on one thing that I miss out on the small details of life. I do the big-picture things well, but sometimes day-to-day tasks get overlooked. One day I ran out of gas in the car—again. I called Bill, who was twenty minutes away, on my cell phone to come rescue me. I left the car about a block from my destination and went to my appointment, knowing that my knight in shining armor would take care of it. However, when Bill arrived at the destination the car was nowhere in sight. He picked me up at my appointment so we could return together to search for the car. We knew that no one could have stolen it—it was out of gas! We were surprised when we called the county sheriff and

MIRROR, MIRROR

"Mirror, mirror, on the wall, who's the fairest of them all?" Our words are mirrors to another's soul. Too often we give those closest to us cracked mirrors of displeasing words or hurtful remarks. These cracked mirrors give a distorted reflection of the person. But when we reflect to those we love their uniqueness and value, they begin to see themselves as priceless.

On our honeymoon, Pam stepped out of the shower and, looking in the mirror, began putting on her makeup. While doing so, she began to verbally criticize her physical attributes. From head to toe, she complained about the way she was put together.

I was lying on the bed admiring Pam when she began her personal evaluation. Inside I was becoming frustrated—after all, she was criticizing my wife!

✿

*I got up and walked toward Pam. I wrapped my arms
around her and gave her a reassuring hug. Then I
stepped back, took her face tenderly in my hands, and
said, "Pam, let me be your mirror. You are gorgeous!
Let me reflect back to you the beautiful woman you
are. If we have to throw all the mirrors in our house
away, we will. From now on, I will be your mirror!"*

Love is like a mirror.
When you love another you become
his mirror and he becomes yours. . . .
And reflecting each other's love
you see infinity.

Leo Buscaglia

✿

they had no record of our car being impounded. We went to pick up our sons at school and called again. Sure enough, the sheriff's department had picked up our car and it would cost us over $100 to get it back!

At this point, I (Bill) had a choice. I could give Pam a difficult time about being oblivious to the gas gauge. Yet she was already having a hard time. She kept apologizing over and over for her mistake. Finally, I stopped the car, looked into her eyes, and said, "Pam, you mean much more to me than that car, and that impound fee is a small price to pay to be in love with you."

That tank of gas cost $147. Accompanied by Bill's kindness, though, it turned out to be a great investment in a very happy, very grateful wife.

It's important to know what to say and when to say it!

Love, like a lamp,
needs to be fed out of the oil
of another's heart,
or its flame burns low.

HENRY WARD BEECHER

❧ WHAT TO SAY ❧

"You're the best!" The one you love will never grow tired of hearing phrases like: *You are amazing! You do that better than anyone I know. You are so talented.* Think about the positive qualities of the one you love and the things he or she does well. What makes your partner unique (her brilliant red hair, his amazing talent with electronics)? Put it in words!

"You can do it!" Everyone feels intimidated or insecure at times. We are frequently bombarded with messages that highlight our insignificance—we're not good enough, not smart enough, or not thin enough. The song "Wind Beneath My Wings" sold millions because it inspired lovers everywhere to consider how high they could soar when someone they love believes in them.

I appreciate getting compliments from people, but when Pam believes in me, I feel like I can conquer the world. Her words hold more weight and have more power to encourage because I value her so much.

> *I like not only to be loved,*
> *but to be told I am loved.*
>
> GEORGE ELIOT

"You matter more!" When Bill changes his schedule for my sake, or when he tells me that being with me is more important than any power lunch, conference, or ball game, I remember it. The words "you matter more" are like a wise investment. Each time you say them to the one you love, more dividends are paid. Then, if you ever have to give gentle correction or you must break a date, you have emotional stock in the bank. The one you love will take the rare negative in stride when you've laid the groundwork with day-after-day statements of love.

Bill delights in making my dreams come true, but often his heart is bigger than his schedule. Sometimes he will volunteer to run by the store or stop at the dry cleaners for me as he runs his other errands, but he also usually forgets at least one of those errands. On one hectic day Bill ran the errands while I finished up some preparation for a marriage conference. When he arrived home I said, "Thanks for getting my clothes at the cleaners, honey." The look on Bill's face told it all. I knew it was too late to get to the cleaners; I wouldn't have the outfit I wanted to wear at the conference. I had a choice. I could get upset at my husband, or I could forgive him and wear another outfit. I knew Bill was for me, so I simply said, "That's okay, sweetheart. I can wear something else. You had a lot to do and something was bound to slip through." I gave him a kiss and packed something else.

Pleasant words are like honey,
sweet to the soul.

THE BOOK OF PROVERBS

❀ ENCOURAGING ACTIONS ❀

The old saying is true. In some ways, opposites do attract. Couples in love often share similar values, interests, and backgrounds. Usually we connect with someone who has a similar emotional past. However, we generally are attracted to someone with a personality different from our own. If we are outgoing and spontaneous, chances are we might be attracted to someone who is stable and organized. If we are quiet and easy-going, we may be attracted to someone with more of a "take-charge" personality. The paradox of being attracted to your opposite is that you may find the things that once attracted you to your sweetheart can, in time, become the things that frustrate you most.

Our friend Sherry is an outgoing people person—but a bit scattered in her carefree approach to life. She was attracted to Kevin's strong, stable, easy-going personality. However, several years into their marriage, Sherry became frustrated with Kevin's lack of spontaneity. "He is so predictable! He's worked the same job. He has the same friends—he seems totally satisfied with the status quo," she lamented to a friend.

Sherry was right—Kevin was content. But he was also content years before she had married him. It was Kevin's easy, comfortable, and secure manner that drew Sherry to him.

One of the most encouraging things Sherry can do is to seek to consistently appreciate the unique personality and gifts that Kevin brings to their relationship. And Sherry can encourage Kevin to try new things by praising and encouraging him. For example, she could say things like, "Kevin, you are so amazing.

Just being with you makes me feel so secure and safe. I'd love to take some ballroom dancing lessons together. I know I'd feel so good being in your arms."

> *All the beautiful sentiments in the world*
> *weigh less than a single lovely action.*
>
> JAMES RUSSELL LOWELL

It's also important to feel emotionally connected to the one we love. I (Pam) am an extrovert—I view life from the outside in. When my life is relatively under control and things are going well, I have the emotional strength I need to give to the ones I love.

I (Bill) am just the opposite. When I sense that I am being respected and valued for being who I am, then I have the strength and motivation to tackle tasks. This difference in our personalities created an ongoing frustration in our lives—organizing our calendars and schedules. Pam loves to consistently coordinate our calendar and review to-do lists. I tend to avoid calendars, even though I know that scheduling is important.

One week it just didn't work for Bill and I to coordinate calendars on Monday, so on Tuesday we worked out together at our gym, then went out to breakfast. Afterward, I asked if we could match calendars. Bill was totally different! He was positive and actually seemed to enjoy the scheduling. I asked him about it and discovered that on Mondays he is tired from his weekend work as a pastor. On Mondays he needs to connect with me on a deep level—beyond scheduling. So I simply rearranged our calendar matching for later on Tuesday and it has worked out great for us.

Find out more about one another. Just talking about your differences and discovering more about each other will encourage you both.

❀ ENCOURAGING GIFTS ❀

Her eyes sparkle as she takes in the box. She notes the store name on the outside and gives you a misty-eyed smile. Carefully she unwraps the package and gently pulls back the delicate tissue paper. She squeals in delight as she unfolds the perfect silk robe, then sighs and flashes you that special smile which says, "You listened . . . you listened to my heart." Pulling the fabric to her cheek to feel its softness, she takes a deep breath, inhaling the perfume of the moment. She throws herself into your arms and wraps her arms around you while she smothers you with kisses—and you know deep down that you did it right!

Familiar acts are beautiful through love.

PERCY BYSSHE SHELLEY

We love giving our loved one the perfect gift. From our first uncertain moments in junior high, poring over items in the discount store, to our dating days of wanting to choose a gift that captures all that we feel for someone special, we long to do it right. Sometimes, year after year, the magic slips away. The practical overtakes the precious. We don't mean for it to

LITTLE MONEY BUT LOTS OF HEART

- Leave a romantic surprise at the bottom of a bubble bath (like a long-stemmed, thornless rose).

- Spray your signature perfume or cologne on his or her pillow and leave a romantic note.

- Instead of a fresh rose, make a rose from two chocolate candy Kisses placed end to end (Kisses wrapped in red foil work best). Attach Kisses to a floral wire and wrap with floral tape. Make a long-stemmed dozen, tie with a big bow, and add a love note—or arrange in a long-stemmed rose box. (Many cities have confectioners who make beautiful chocolate roses.)

- Write a passionate note on a steamy mirror.

- On a rainy day, write a love note and place it in a plastic sandwich bag. Tie it to the windshield wiper on your lover's car for a rainy-day surprise.

- Try dance lessons for the two of you—
  in your living room.

- Send a singing telegram—you do the singing!

- Place an "I love you" message in a public place
  (an ad in the personals, a yard sign, a song
  dedicated on the radio, etc.).

- Give gift certificates for favorites: an
  hour-long massage by you, a weekend trip,
  breakfast in bed, etc.

- To create personalized romantic stationery, use
  beautiful photo pages out of magazines and write
  a note over the photo.

- Tuck those perfumed pages in magazines into a
  drawer for the scent of romance in unexpected places.

- Do a mundane chore for the one you love and
  leave a surprise after you've completed it. For
  example, fill up the gas tank, then leave a candy
  Kiss or a Mon Cherie on the steering wheel.

happen. Didn't she say that the toaster was broken? Didn't he mention he needed a belt to go with his brown slacks?

Finding the perfect gift is an art—the art of keen observation, the art of listening to the heart, not just the words. By observing and listening we can find that perfect gift.

Observe the Past. When Christmas arrives, watch how the one you love reacts to gifts that others receive. Do collectibles make her ooh and aah? Is it the sacrificial love of a handmade quilt or jewelry box? Is it the expensive item that he would never buy for himself? Is it the wonder of a surprise gift that's just what she longed for? Is it the sentimental? The simple? The sublime? As soon as you can steal away to somewhere quiet, make a few notes on gifts that warmed the heart of the one you love. *Write it down!*

Observe the Collection. Does the person you love collect certain items? These people make gift giving so much easier. If they collect a certain artist's work, spoons from around the world, old-fashioned tins, music boxes, or even vintage comic books or cookbooks—note the collection. Some people don't collect on purpose but may have a collection that others have started for them. I think of my friend Kitty. You guessed it—everyone in her life gives her cats. Wooden cats, ceramic cats, cat pot holders, cat magnets, cat paintings—all sorts of cats adorn Kitty's house.

My grandfather loved to listen to Paul Harvey on the radio. He always laughed at the surprise endings of Harvey's "Rest of the Story" monologues. Everyone who visited Grandpa's house saw how he loved to laugh—so year after year people gave him things to encourage that wonderful laughter. He displays joke books, comic books, funny statues, gag gifts, and humorous poems and cards. He never set out to collect funny things, but it was obvious to everyone who loved him that the ideal present for Gerald was a funny gift.

Observe the Dream. As you find yourself strolling hand in hand along the beach or through a cute shop, ask questions to find out those hidden dreams or goals of the one you love. One year, Bill really wanted to encourage my heart. I was a reentry woman finishing a bachelor's degree, and I wanted to succeed at writing. That year I got fun writing helps (like a thesaurus, a writer's magazine, a pretty pen, a journal) in my Christmas stocking and on Valentine's Day. For my birthday, he put a soft nightie in a briefcase. It was the perfect way to say, "I believe in your dream. I believe in you. Yet I will always want you to be close to my heart and in my arms." Another gift that says "I believe in your dream" may not be useable immediately but a gesture that looks ahead, such as reservations at a conference, tickets to a traveling ballet, or chore or errand coupons that can be redeemed to provide guilt-free time to pursue a dream or hobby.

Observe the Daily. Clues to the desires of your loved one's heart may be revealed on random notes tucked into books or dog-eared pages in a mail-order catalog. For daily encouragement, Pam places motivational sayings and favorite Bible verses on brightly colored pieces of paper around our mirror. A small leadership group she was leading wanted to give her a thank-you gift. They called me to ask for suggestions. I knew that Pam had just purchased business cards, so I suggested a business-card holder for her purse. On the cover was her favorite verse from the bathroom mirror, "The Lord is my strength, He makes my feet like Hind's [deer] feet and makes me walk on my high places." Pam tells me that each time she hands out a business card, she remembers how thoughtful her leadership group was and how caring I was to notice her everyday needs.

Observe the Anxiety. The perfect gift is often one that renews and rejuvenates. One year, I knew Bill's schedule was particularly busy. I know that physical exercise is the best medicine for him when he is on a tight schedule. So I bought a gym bag, a Walkman, and fun sports clothes, and created his own personal relaxation package. A delightful gift for women is baskets filled with fragrant bath accessories. Those gifts say, "Someone noticed everything that I do and they appreciate me enough to give me a special time to relax and unwind!"

Observe the Risk. Sometimes you have to go out on a limb and take a chance on a gift. Despite the uncertainty, these gifts can be the hit of a lifetime! Try the outrageous—two tickets for bungee jumping, a totally funky work of art that matches your personality in a unique way, tickets to something fun and goofy (like to a log-rolling contest or frog-jumping event). These risky gifts work best when given with a "sure thing" gift—like dessert at your favorite restaurant or a romantic book of poetry.

Observe the Happily-Ever-After Stories. Yes, many women really *do* like to ride in a horse-drawn carriage like Cinderella or have Prince Charming ride up and whisk them away on a white horse. Many women love the thought of running across a meadow of daisies and into the arms of her true love. If her favorite movie is *Sleepless in Seattle,* meet her atop the Empire State Building for a date! (Or at least buy her the movie soundtrack!)

Some romantic plots work time and again—like greeting her at the door with a bouquet of fresh flowers. It's a sure way to your loved one's heart!

Let us not love with words . . .
but with actions.

THE BOOK OF 1 JOHN

Observe the Practical. Be on the lookout for the perfect gift—and be prepared! Write down the sizes of everything your loved one wears, from shoes to hat to ring—and everything in between. Carry that list with you at all times. You never know when you'll see that matchless something. Make note of favorite clothing styles and colors, his or her signature perfume or cologne, names and numbers of her makeup consultant or his fishing supply store. The perfect person to ask about the ideal gift is the retailer who has done business with your partner all year. Your sweetheart may have inadvertently said something like, "Oh, I'd love to have that, but it's so expensive. I could never afford it." Go buy that very item!

Observe the Sentimental. Bill has noticed that every year on Christmas and Mother's Day I get into a "Victorian" mood. It's like clockwork. I may be practical and efficient all year, but at Christmas and on Mother's Day my heart longs for dainty flowered teacups, intricate lacework, and charming antiques! A sure gift is anything that nurtures my Victorian mood!

In observing the sentimental, you might notice that he keeps the broken pocket watch his dad handed down to him, or she has heirloom jewelry that she never wears. You might seek out a talented framer and have these cherished items displayed in a shadow box. Our friend Marjorie lost nearly all her worldly goods in a house fire several years ago. A few items survived because they were buried deep in a drawer: some of her own baby clothes, treasured family photos, the sax her son played, and some of his sheet music. She had these precious items matted, framed, and accented with dried flowers and other small touches. Now two wonderful framed memories hang proudly in her new home.

Observe the Day. A gift sure to please is the gift of your time. Set aside an entire day to celebrate your lover. This works best if it happens on a day that isn't a birthday, anniversary, or Christmas. Choose a day you can work out with your partner's schedule and make it a surprise by whisking him or her away from work! Give your sweetheart your full attention. Seek to meet his or her requests all day. Compliment his or her talents and be considerate of any emotional needs. Top off the day with a poem or song written especially for him, or fix her a candlelight dinner while she soaks lazily in the bubble bath. Celebrate your love!

In pleasure's dream, or sorrow's hour,
In crowded hall or lonely bower,
The business of my soul shall be
Forever to remember thee!

BEN FRANKLIN

ENCOURAGING GIFTS

Being an artist at romance does not require so much a sentimental and emotional nature as it requires a thoughtful nature. When we think of the romantic things, we think of events that occur because someone made a choice to love. A man stops off at a florist and brings his wife a single rose in the evening, a girl makes her lover a lemon pie with just the degree of tartness he likes, a wife makes arrangements for her husband to take the caribou-hunting trip he thought he'd never afford—these are not the goo of sweet emotion, they are the stuff that comes from resolution and determination, and they are strong mortar.

ALAN LOY MCGINNIS
The Romance Factor

TRADITIONS AND MEMORIES TO MAKE LOVE LAST

The Photo Shoot. Have a friend show up to take pictures of a surprise date. Or stop by a photo booth and take those old-fashioned black-and-white shots that print out in a long strip. You could even hire a professional photographer to drop by your dinner table for a photo session. Here in San Diego we have a company that comes to the location of your date. They take some paparazzi shots, then sneak in an interview. A few days later you receive a front page article about your date!

Roll 'Em. Have a friend videotape your special moments together and edit them into a film starring the two of you! Another version of this is to videotape a message from yourself to your loved one and send it prior to a big date. Let the anticipation build.

I Love to Hear Your Voice. We vacationed in Hawaii for our fifteenth wedding anniversary.

When we returned to the States, I wanted Bill to remember how nice it was to be "just us." I purchased a photo frame that also had the capacity to record a message. I recorded a message for his ears only that was full of innuendo and secret messages. I slid in a romantic picture of us under a waterfall, wrapped the gift, and slid it into his desk drawer at work. He loved the surprise! And I loved the memories it brought back as I created it.

The Ornament. No matter where we travel on our yearly anniversary getaway, we always purchase a Christmas ornament. Each year when we decorate our tree, we reminisce over those good times together. Other versions of this are mug collections, gift spoons, baseball caps, t-shirts, or music CDs. Anything that will renew fun memories and bring a smile to your face will do.

The Journal. Record precious thoughts, memorable dialogue, and special conversations into a journal. After you write down the facts, add your musings, poetry, or artwork. Choose a journal with an elegant cover or create your own padded-fabric cover.

A-a-ahh, the Taste of It. *Enjoy the same favorite snack, chocolate treat, or other luscious delicacy that you enjoyed during a special time together. Every time we taste kiwi or guava, we feel like we've returned to the Hawaiian Islands. Each time we drink hot apple cider, we recall a midnight sleigh ride through snowy fields. Strawberries remind us of picnics, and bunches of grapes bring back memories of carefree days spent on California beaches. Cherries Jubilee is our anniversary tradition!*

The Aroma. *Like tastes, good smells can bring back precious memories. I have an aftershave that I buy for Bill especially for our anniversary. The aroma of coffee wafting through the house still hints of our December honeymoon spent in cold but cozy Lake Tahoe. Pine trees elicit remembrances of days spent relaxing together at Hume Lake in the*

Sequoia National Forest. Sea air will forever bring
back memories of the first real heart-to-heart talk we
had as we sat on Morro Rock in Morro Bay.
We watched the waves break against the rock while
the sea stretched out forever in front of us—
two nineteen-year-olds in love.

So Soft. Invest in things that invoke memories
of soft, romantic days. It feels wonderful to come
home after a long, hard day and wrap up together
in a cozy afghan or handmade quilt. I like to wear
Bill's warm down jacket to help ease my loneliness
when he's traveling. You may want to buy matching
moccasins on that next trip to the southwest or
satin sheets in New Orleans.

By gently including each of the five senses into our
traditions and daily lives, we enhance our ability to
recall and cherish those special moments together.

CHAPTER 2

Can You Hear My Heart?

GAIN A DEEPER LOVE THROUGH UNDERSTANDING

God has put something noble and good into every heart which his hand created.

MARK TWAIN

IT WILL BE IMPOSSIBLE FOR ME TO EVER FULLY understand what it is like to be a man—I'm not one! The only way I'll ever discover the joys and challenges that are a part of a man's life is to learn from Bill.

Likewise, it is impossible for me (Bill) to understand what it is like to be a woman. The only way I will understand a woman's needs and desires is to encourage Pam to share hers with me.

Men and women are different! Once we understand that, we can delight in those differences. And they can draw our hearts together more intimately.

❀ WAFFLES AND SPAGHETTI ❀

When it comes to the way men and women think, we are radically different. We like to say that men are like waffles and women are like spaghetti. Let's take a look at men first. Men compartmentalize life, focusing on one thing at a time. It's like this—when you look at a waffle, you see lots of individual boxes with walls in between them. Men deal with life as if their brains contained a waffle. They take one issue and put it in a box, then take the next issue and place it in another separate box. If we could see a man's thoughts, they would look just like a waffle, with each little box holding an individual area of life. This causes men to do only one thing at a time. When men are at work, they are at work. When men are doing yardwork, they are doing yardwork. When men are fishing, they are fishing. And when your loved one is thinking about being intimate with you, that's all he's thinking about!

Women, on the other hand, experience life more like a plate of spaghetti. If you look at a plate of spaghetti, you imme-diately notice that everything touches everything else. That is how women think—they connect every issue. Women have this incredible ability to deal with everything simultaneously. Since it is impossible to fix everything and have it all under control, women fit everything in life together emotionally, feeling something about each issue in their lives. Women may feel happy emotions like sentimentality, joy, and enthusiasm, or they may feel sad emotions like depression or frustration. But the key is to experience *some* emotion. Once women have emotionally connected with each issue in their lives, they will relax and begin to enjoy the world around them. Women are terrific at combining things. In the same half hour, they can call a friend, plan a special dinner, run a business meeting, write a Christmas card, check in with the kids, and not miss a beat!

Oh, the tension this waffle-and-spaghetti dilemma can cause in our relationships! She begins a conversation. He thinks this discussion is about the first issue she brings up. About the time he starts offering a solution to her problem, she changes the subject. He offers more insightful answers, and she changes the subject again! *Is she deliberately trying to dodge my help*, he thinks, *or is she just an irrational creature?*

He begins a conversation, and she gets all excited because she has been waiting for him to open up to her. As he shares his concerns, her mind kicks into gear and she comes up with eight other areas of life related to this one. In an attempt to help, she encourages him to consider the outcome of this discussion for his family, friends, and future success. He suddenly stops the conversation and stands up. With discouragement in his voice, he says, "You have never understood me." *He just doesn't know how to communicate,* she thinks.

So what do you do?

A Love Fort for Two

Listen to one another's hearts as you hide out in a love fort built for two. Use your childhood imagination and rearrange your living room furniture into your own private fort. Invite the one you love to camp out with you. Here are some provisions for a fun evening hideout—

- sleeping bags and pillows
- peanut butter and jelly sandwiches
- thermos of milk to accompany the sandwiches
- 2 bags of Tootsie Roll Pops—see whose bag lasts the longest!
- 1 flashlight—share it to keep close to each other
- travel books for looking and dreaming
- caramel corn to munch on while flipping through travel books
- bottled water to quench your thirst
- cherry chapstick—for lots of kissing!

Combine the adventure of childhood with the beauty of romance as you laugh, share, and keep close.

LOVE FORT CARAMEL CORN

2 c. brown sugar

1 c. corn syrup

$^1/_2$ c. butter

$^1/_2$ Tbsp. baking soda

1 tsp. vanilla

1 tsp. salt

Stir together well sugar, syrup, salt, and butter. Heat
until it boils, stirring constantly. Boil approximately
5 more minutes (soft ball stage). Remove from heat,
add soda and vanilla. Pour over popcorn.
(Good for about 5 to 6 quarts of popcorn.)

❧ TAKE TURNS ❧

The first key to enjoying both waffles *and* spaghetti is to take turns leading the conversation. When the discussion is female-oriented, men need to get ready to take a verbal journey. Know that she will change subjects regularly and explore many ideas before the discussion is over! It's like she's traveling around a plate of spaghetti, switching directions each time two issues meet. This is how her conversation might go:

Hey, honey, how is your truck running? I passed by your favorite auto parts store the other day because I was at the dress shop that is just down the street from it. I was looking at this really cute dress that I was thinking about buying. They didn't have the color I wanted, so I decided not to buy it. But the one in the window was this really pretty mauve color—you know, the same color dress the president's wife was wearing when we saw her on television the other night. Did you think her views on public education were accurate? I just don't know. I sometimes worry about what our kids are learning at school.

As she takes off on her verbal trip, you are wondering what the First Lady's dress has to do with your pick-up truck. But just let her flow in seamless conversation, and you will be amazed at how much understanding she will attribute to you. Actively listen as she leads the journey, and don't try to figure her out.

When the discussion is male-oriented, women need to prepare themselves to stay put and focus on the issue at hand. As a man explores the single issue that is on his mind, he will discover needs behind that issue. As he gets in touch with the needs that motivate his behavior, his lover will feel closer to him and gain satisfying insight into his life. The important thing to remember is that a man takes awhile to discover these needs on his own. He needs the help of a patient, interested partner to help him learn about himself. She needs to encourage him to be open and talk deeply!

May your love increase
and overflow for each other . . .

THE BOOK OF 1 THESSALONIANS

❄ DON'T FIX; JUST LEARN ❄

It's one of the great mysteries of life. Members of the opposite sex need one another, but they don't always have the answers for each other. Men aren't women and women aren't men! But, as we learn to take risks and open up to each other, we will learn and grow both individually and as a couple. Share your heart with the one you love!

❄ ENJOY YOUR DIFFERENCES ❄

I was reminded of how different I am from Pam when I went fishing one day. My fishing buddy and I spent six hours on the glorious Pacific Ocean. We were thrilled to think of ourselves as two men conquering the sea—just us against the life of the ocean. After our trip, I came home to share the spoils of war with my wife—two small fish that barely put up a fight.

The first thing Pam asked me was, "So, what did the two of you talk about?"

GEMS OF LOVE

Whether you're celebrating a wedding anniversary, engagement, or just being together, the message is the same—your loved one is a gem, one worthy of your praise and adoration. You can give your sweetheart a sparkling gem or—if you cannot afford jewels—a poem from your heart about your jewel is just as priceless.

Some traditional meanings of various gems—

- Amethyst—sincerity
- Diamond—sparkling love, sentiment, tradition, innocence, light
- Emerald—success in love
- Garnet—truth, constancy
- Opal—confidence, happiness, hope, innocence, prayer, tender love
- Pearl—perfect beauty, faithfulness, humility, innocence, integrity, modest splendor, moonlight, purity, rarity, refinement, patience, self-sacrifice, wealth, wisdom
- Ruby—beauty, charity, daintiness, dignity, happiness, light, love, passion
- Sapphire—calmness, constancy, contemplation, heaven, hope, innocence, purity, truth, virtue, wisdom
- Topaz—divine goodness, eager love, fidelity, friendship, gentleness, integrity, uprightness, triumph
- Turquoise—harmony

Rings have long been exchanged as beloved tokens of love. Circular rings have symbolized eternal love since the days of the early Egyptians.

Engraved messages on rings became popular during Shakespeare's time. Some early inscriptions read: "I will be yours while life endures"; "In thee my choice do I rejoice"; and "Love in the small but perfect circle trace, and duty in its soft but strict embrace."

In the eighteenth and nineteenth century, lovers gave each other rings set with precious stones that spelled out messages such as "dearest" (Diamond, Emerald, Amethyst, Ruby, Epidote, Sapphire, Turquoise).

Rings made of gold traditionally symbolize a noble union.

If you're searching for a ring for the one you love, incorporate an old custom into the giving of it—have a message engraved, choose a stone for its meaning, or write a poem about your endless love.

"Fishing."

"The whole six hours you were out there all you talked about was fishing?"

"No, we only talked for about two hours."

"Well," she asked, "what did you do the rest of your time?"

With an astonished look on my face, I said, "We fished."

She just looked at me with an amused smile, so I asked her, "Well, if you and your friend had been out on the boat for six hours, how long would the two of you have talked?"

"Six hours," she said without hesitation.

"What in the world would you have talked about for that long?"

"Not fishing!" she exclaimed with a grin.

Yes, it would have been a different fishing trip with Pam and her friend aboard. But differences work well for a couple because you each need each other's strengths. You need both focus and nurturing in your relationship, as well as variety. And when a couple is connected emotionally, the results are fantastic! I married Pam because my own company was not enough. I didn't need to find someone just like me. I wanted someone who brought new interests and a fresh perspective into my life. And the joy of being close to someone who is different than me is wonderfully fulfilling.

When we expect the same from each other, it's like pouring spaghetti sauce on waffles or pancake syrup on spaghetti.

Who wants to eat maple-flavored spaghetti or waffles marinara? No one we know! But when spaghetti is covered with steaming, spicy sauce, it's hard to contain your desire to feast. When waffles are dripping with maple syrup or topped with whipped cream and strawberries, you can hardly hold yourself back from diving in and devouring them. Have a romantic banquet with each other by simmering your differences together.

> *There is no remedy for love*
> *but to love more.*
>
> HENRY DAVID THOREAU

❀ TRUST ONE ANOTHER ❀

As a team, you make a winning combination. You are each suited for success in different things. In our relationship, Pam is much better at organizing the kids' schedules and Bill is much better at organizing the finances. Because of our differences, we divide the responsibilities in our relationship based on our waffle-and-spaghetti differences. Pam gets to be in charge of the things that need to be fit together. Bill is in charge of anything that requires long-term concentration. For example, Pam organizes our schedules, plans and leads family devotions, coordinates our goals, arranges child-care, and oversees household chores. Bill services the cars, handles the finances, oversees yardwork, and maintains the house and all of our equipment. As a team, we use our differences to accomplish great things!

It could be disastrous if we switched roles. If Bill were in charge of schedules there would be very little future planning—and some missed meetings! If Pam were in charge of our automobiles, we would probably be walking.

The key to making this arrangement work is trusting each other. I have to believe that Pam will keep my best interests in mind when she coordinates the schedules for our family of five. I need to make my schedule flexible for family activities and check with her before I make any commitments of my own.

On the other hand, I need to trust Bill with the regular financial decisions of our life. I tend to handle the checkbook in a creative way, finding money we don't have. I need to believe that Bill's plan for paying our bills is right for us as a couple, and I need to check with him before making any major purchases. I can't assume we have money just because we got a paycheck!

Men and women *are* different. But those differences make life interesting, rich, and complete. When we seek to understand one another, talk about our differences heart to heart, and support one another in these differences, we gain a deeper love.

Love seeks one thing only:
the good of the one loved.
It leaves all other secondary effects
to take care of themselves.
Love, therefore, is its own reward.

THOMAS MERTON

WAFFLES FOR HIM

Serve breakfast in bed to your husband. Add a note that says, "It's okay. I'll stay in any waffle box you need me to—however long you need me to!"

Whole Wheat and Pecan Waffles

1 ½ c. sifted whole-wheat flour

¾ tsp. salt

2 tsp. baking powder

2 eggs separated

1 ½ c. milk

5 Tbsp. oil

2 Tbsp. sugar

Sift flour, salt, and baking powder together twice. Beat egg yolks until light. Add milk, sugar, and oil. Add dry ingredients until they are just blended. Fold in stiffly beaten egg whites. (Only stir a little.) Pour into hot, pregreased waffle iron. Spoon on pecans. Bake until done.

—Recipe from Pam's hometown in Idaho

SPAGHETTI SAUCE FOR HER

Serve with a rose in a vase and a note that says, "Honey, I love you. I will listen—really listen— and go on a journey with you."

Saute garlic in olive oil (about 2 to 3 cloves, minced in about 1 Tbsp. of olive oil)

2 cans tomato paste (approx. 24 oz. total)

2 to 3 fresh tomatoes or a small can of diced tomatoes (fresh tomatoes are preferred)

1 large can of tomato puree

Add together, then add enough water to make the sauce as thick as cream.

add:

2 tsp. salt (add in a little at a time, and taste as you go)

black pepper to taste

$^1/_2$ tsp. oregano—crushed

$^1/_2$ to $^3/_4$ tsp. basil (If you use fresh basil, don't add until the end. Do not cook fresh basil.)

Cook and stir until it gently ripples (not a boil), then lower heat and simmer at least 2 $^1/_2$ hours.

Variation: In an oven or fry pan, brown Italian sausage and add to sauce and simmer. You can either add it whole or you can cut it up and add it—great flavor!

This recipe has been handed down from mother to daughter in a wonderful Italian family.

—Grace Holtz

CHAPTER 3

Heart-to-Heart Talk

COMMUNICATION THAT CONNECTS

Love each other warmly,
with all your heart.

THE BOOK OF 1 PETER

THE FIRE WAS BLAZING IN THE FIREPLACE, WARMING the room and casting a romantic glow upon us. We sat curled up in each other's laps. For hours, Bill and I sat and talked— really talked. Hopes, dreams, loves, cherished moments—our hearts connected on a deep and wonderful level. After seventeen years together, these times are still so special to us.

All of us long to be known—really known and accepted by the one we love. As lovers, we must capture those moments together in the busyness of day-to-day life.

❀ GETTING TO THE HEART OF THINGS ❀

We talk to each other in many ways, communicating in layers. Starting with small talk, we work to deeper topics by communicating things like, "Brian has a dentist appointment at ten. Can you take him?" or "I like the blue wallpaper better." As we talk, we reveal more of our own thoughts, opinions, and feelings. At each level of conversation we seek affirmation and acceptance. We open up to each other in new and wonderful ways as we listen and share.

Engage in Small Talk: This is that tidbits kind of talk like, "Got a letter from Mom today" or "Kerry has a doctor appointment at two." Relationships need a lot of this kind of conversation. Every day couples have to relay bits and pieces of information back and forth—but there's much more to communication than small talk!

Explore New Ideas: Ideas can be liked or disliked, embraced or dismissed. If we attach any of ourselves to our ideas, sharing them is a little like stepping out on an icy pond. But great things can happen when couples explore their ideas!

Share Your Opinions: Opinions carry emotions, bits of ourselves, our beliefs, values, and convictions. Good relationships value the free expression of opinions. Learn to seek out each other's opinions!

Move on to Emotional Sharing: Emotional sharing carries our hearts. It makes us "feel" like we're in love. We share at this level when we think, "It's like he knows me!" or "We just connected!" or "We stayed up and talked till three in the morning!"

$\mathcal{B}$EYOND

Beyond words

or phrases

or prose penned

Beyond the lines and meter

and rhythm

and rhyme

Beyond a syllable whispered

or sound released

Language cannot reach

the place where your love

has carried me.

PAM FARREL

How do I love thee? Let me count the ways.
I love thee to the depth and breadth and height
My soul can reach, when feeling out of sight
For the ends of Being and ideal Grace.
I love thee to the level of everyday's
Most quiet need, by sun and candle-light.
I love thee freely, as men strive for Right;
I love thee purely, as they turn from Praise.
I love thee with the passion put to use
In my old griefs, and with my childhood's faith.
I love thee with a love I seemed to lose
With my lost saints,—I love thee with the breath,
Smiles, tears, of all my life!—and, if God choose,
I shall but love thee better after death.

ELIZABETH BARRETT BROWNING

It is emotional sharing that best strengthens a relationship. Take time to share on this level during a quiet evening by the fire, a peaceful mountain hike, or an afternoon picnic in a sunny meadow. Listen to your loved one's heart, then share your own.

What makes a great heart-to-heart talk, one where you and your partner talk openly and deeply?

Be Interested. Turn face to face. Hold hands. Lean toward each other. Put down the paper, turn off the television, and face the heart of the one who is sharing. You will connect deeply— heart to heart.

Repeat It. Repeat the key phrases as your loved one talks with you. By repeating these things, your conversation will go deeper as the one you love expands on his or her thoughts and feelings. Take time to find out the little details. If you keep repeating things back and encouraging more sharing, you might soon be exchanging intimate thoughts, hopes, and dreams.

It is best to listen much and speak little.

THE BOOK OF JAMES

Work for Understanding. Try to understand by giving back your version of what has been shared. For example, "What I hear you saying is that you're feeling really stressed about work. Are you afraid you might not get that promotion?" Then give your love an opportunity to respond and say "Yes, that's right" or "No, not quite." Further your understanding by asking questions that require a deeper answer, like, "When you think about not getting that promotion, how does it make you feel?" Understand by asking!

Relate to One Another. Try to connect the thought or situation to something you might have felt or experienced. By connecting your experience to your loved one's, you are expressing a desire to understand and empathize. Never say, "I know exactly what you are feeling." You don't. You only know what is being expressed to you and how you would feel in that situation—they may or may not be the same feelings. Check out those emotions by asking caring questions, then try to feel what they feel.

Let love be your greatest aim.

THE BOOK OF 1 CORINTHIANS

Recapture It. Use passwords to get your conversation flowing again after you've been sidetracked. Passwords are words or phrases the two of you agree on that encourage you to get back on track. They can be humorous or nostalgic, but they always have special meaning to both you and your loved one. Passwords remind you that this relationship is important and that you are both committed to making it work.

Recently, I found a way to handle a situation that had been frustrating me for years. I am a one-task-at-a-time man who likes to start a project and finish it before I begin another. When I feel myself getting overwhelmed with the responsibilities of my life, I take a break from new ideas and focus on just one issue. This helps me relax and prepare for the next round

THE PAGES OF LOVE

Go on a date to your favorite book shop or the
local library. Choose one of these romantic books to
read snuggled together by the fireplace or curled up
with each other on the porch swing.

The poetry of Elizabeth Barrett Browning
and Robert Browning

Love Poems *(published by Alfred Knopf Publishers,
edited by Peter Washington)*

Great Love Poems *(Dover Thrift Edition)*

Love Letters: An Anthology of Passion *by
Michelle Lovric (Shooting Star Press)*

Anne of Green Gables *by L.M. Montgomery
(or Anne's House of Dreams, which is considered
by some to be the "most romantic" Anne book)*

The Lady of Shalott *by Alfred, Lord Tennyson*

A Room with a View *by E.M. Forster
(or Howard's End)*

Emma *by Jane Austen (or any Austen book)*

Jane Eyre *by Charlotte Brontë*

Rebecca *by Daphne du Maurier*

of responsibility. Pam, on the other hand, is an idea person. She pumps out ideas like sunshine. Pam relaxes by coming up with and discussing new ideas and, unlike me, she thinks up new ideas to relieve stress.

Oftentimes, when we were sitting around relaxing together, Pam would begin to share a long list of inspirational ideas about how to make the world a better place. As I listened to her endless stream of ideas, I found myself getting tired. I finally realized that I was getting overwhelmed because I felt as if I needed to act on every one of these ideas! But I didn't— Pam just wanted to share her thoughts with me and have me understand her.

Love does not demand its own way . . .
Love is not irritable or touchy.

THE BOOK OF 1 CORINTHIANS

That was when the light went on for me. For the first time in fifteen years of marriage, I realized I didn't have to feel responsible for every idea Pam came up with. When we were newlyweds, it was flattering to me to be able to take her ideas and make them happen. After we had children, it became harder. I now felt as if a big weight had been taken off my shoulders. I asked Pam, "When you are sharing ideas that I really don't think I can act on, may I say, 'Pam, that is a great idea!'?"

You can't imagine my relief when she said, "I think that is a great idea!"

"That is a great idea" has become a password in our relationship that carries a good deal of meaning for us. Whenever one of us uses this phrase, it makes us laugh but it also is a compliment to the creativity and ambition that we both appreciate in each other.

Here are some fun ways to find your own password:

• *Think of your favorite commercials.* One couple discovered that they both liked Hallmark commercials so their password became, "We care enough to send the very best." By saying this, they were also saying to each other, "I'm trying to say it right, but it just isn't coming out like a greeting card. Can we try again?"

• *Talk about your favorite cartoons or jokes.* Humor is an effective password. One couple's personalities were very opposite. She was quiet and he was like the Road Runner—always going 100 mph. So their password became "Beep, beep!" They were telling each other, "Slow down. Don't try to fix me—listen to me."

• *Think of your favorite movies or books.* Early in our marriage, one of our passwords was a bad joke that Bill quoted from the original *Rocky* movie. Any time I was depressed or melodramatic, Bill would say in his not-very-good Rocky impersonation, "You know what you get when you tap a turtle on the back? Shell shock. Get it? Shell shock." It would always make me laugh. We used it so often that sometimes he would

THE ECHO

I shouted aloud and louder
While out on the plain one day;
The sound grew faint and fainter
Until it had died away.
My words had gone forever.
They left no trace or track,
But the hills nearby caught up the cry
And sent an echo back.

I spoke a word in anger
To one who was my friend,
Like a knife it cut him deeply,
A wound that was hard to mend.
That word, so thoughtlessly
uttered, I would we could both forget,

But its echo lives and

memory gives

The recollection yet.

How many hearts are broken,

How many friends are lost

By some unkind word spoken

Before we count the cost!

But a word or deed of kindness

Will repay a hundredfold,

For it echoes again in the heart of men

And carries a joy untold.

C.A. LUFBURROW

just tap his wrist a certain way, and I'd know that he was talking about that turtle!

Looking for a fun way out of the miscommunication whirlwind? Try your own special password.

Take time to really talk with each other. Share your hopes and dreams. Delight in your different ways of looking at the world. Come together heart to heart.

You soothe my soul, you fill it with so tender a sentiment that it is sweet to live . . .

JULIE DE L'ESPINASSE

PENNING A TIMELESS LOVE LETTER

Love letters carry a special place in romance. The words can be read over and over. The one you love can feel connected even if you are miles apart. A love letter can bridge a disagreement, lay a foundation for the future, and rekindle the passion of a first date or honeymoon. A love letter also slows down the pace of life and gives your loved one a tender place to rest— in the beauty of your words.

The best love letters are the ones that contain a few key ingredients—sincerity, sentiment, and expectation.

Express Sincerity: Talk from your heart. Tell the one you love why you love him or her. Write songs or poetry, or try listing the alphabet A to Z on a sheet of pretty paper, then think of words beginning with each letter that capture the wonderful person your loved one is. You can also do this by taking the letters of their name to form a note. For example, we might write to each other:

Perky

Alluring

Marvelous

or

Best

Indescribable

Living

Lover

The first is a list of character qualities.
The second example is a sentence: Bill is the best
indescribable living lover.

In a love letter, go on and on about how empty your
life would be without him or her. Or show how dis-
tracted being in love is for you. Simone de Beauvoir
wrote to her lover, "I'm altogether immersed in the hap-
piness I derive from seeing you. Nothing else counts."

❋

Robert and Elizabeth Browning are the ultimate
poetic lovers. They have thrilled and inspired lovers
with lines like:

"You have lifted my very soul up into the light
of your soul, and I am not ever likely to
mistake it for the common daylight."
Elizabeth to Robert,
August 17, 1846.

"All my soul follows you, love—encircles
you—and I live in being yours."
Robert to Elizabeth,
January 28, 1846.

Elizabeth's poem "How Do I Love Thee? Let Me Count
the Ways" is a model for exactly what a love letter should
do—recount all the ways you love your beloved.

Express Sentiment: You can use some simple
writing tools to express your love on paper.
Here are a few things to try:

❋

Describe Your Love: "*O, my love is like a red, red rose . . .*" reads a romantic line from a Robert Burns poem. For a great example of counting the ways you love, read the Song of Songs, "*Your eyes are like doves . . . your lips are like a scarlet thread . . .*" Imagine creative ways to describe the love you share.

Through My Eyes: *Show your love by telling your loved one how he or she rates in your life—at the top! I often say to Bill, "You're the best!" And I truly mean that he is the greatest at everything in my eyes. You might write, "You have the prettiest eyes in the whole wide world" or "Nobody smiles like you do."*

Poetic Compliments: *A compliment that compares your loved one to something precious, costly, or desirable is always a good addition to a love letter. Most women would love to be compared to a rose, a priceless jewel, a sparkling waterfall, or a brilliant rainbow. You can also compare your mate to* something not necessarily beautiful but complimentary nonetheless. For example, I often say to Pam, "You're a rock!" By this, I am complimenting Pam's character. She can persist in difficult circumstances with confidence and grace.

A Pledge of Love: *Lovers share everything with each other—especially themselves.* Dorothy Osborne wrote to her future husband, Sir William Temple, "My very dreams are yours." George Farquhar wrote to Anne Oldfield: "I have told you my passion, my eyes have spoke it, my tongue pronounced it, and my pen declared it. Now my heart is full of you, my head raves of you, and my hand writes to you." Without spelling it out, George is pledging his time, talent, and very person in pursuit of this love!

You can write stirring love letters. You can begin with a love note like this one:

My Dearest _____,

I love you because (think of two or three
heartwarming reasons). When I see (something
beautiful for women, something strong for men),
I think of you because (describe how they are beautiful
or strong). You are the greatest. I want to (give a
creative suggestion for how you want to love
him or her), and when I think of you it makes me
(describe an emotion—fulfilled, blessed, overjoyed).
I love being with you. I love your (share everything
you adore about him or her). And you are just as
(say how you feel about your loved one's heart—
wonderful, marvelous) inside. You are so incredibly
(honest, fair, caring). I am yours forever.

With all my love,

(Sign your name with a flourish)

Get a fancy pen, beautiful stationery, and
perfume or cologne to dab on the stationery,
and let your heart speak!

Something happens to our thoughts and emotions
when we put them into a letter; they are then not the
same as spoken words. They are placed in a different,
special context, and they speak at a different level. . . .

THOMAS MOORE

CHAPTER 4

Creative Heart

IDEAS TO KEEP PLENTY
OF PIZZAZZ IN YOUR LOVE

My heart is ever at your service.

WILLIAM SHAKESPEARE

HOW CAN YOU SURPRISE THE ONE YOU LOVE ON HIS OR her birthday? When Valentine's Day is just around the corner, how can you add a little zip to your love life? And how can you create delightful memories of "just for fun" times together? Life and love don't have to become routine with each passing year. Try these fun relationship enhancers to keep the flame of love burning brightly:

Look Back: Try a date that revisits some of those first memories of your relationship. Journey back to the place you first met, first kissed, or where your first heart-to-heart talk happened. Or you can bring that trip to you—pack a picnic together, look through a photo album of your early times together, and reminisce. Put "your" song in the CD player and take a drive to your old neighborhood, high school or college, or favorite restaurant. Maybe this is the time to renew your commitment to each other. Looking back can help nurture those feelings that first drew you together, and it can remind you both of all the memories you have given each other.

Look Ahead: We both keep lists of "dream dates" that we'd love to go on. Once a year, we remake our lists and give them to each other as a gift. We also give each other a love list of ten free things that make us feel loved. Having these lists helps us surprise one another on a regular basis. By looking ahead, you can also plan to invest in your relationship by attending a seminar, conference, or retreat. You might also buy your loved one a gift that says, "I love the person you are becoming. I'm excited about your life—and ours together. I just wanted you to know that I believe in your dream." When a couple will cherish each other's dreams and goals, they can delight in falling in love over and over again.

Seize the Moment: Show your love now. Practice the art of touch. Reach over and hold her hand, give him a squeeze, pat her back. If you're within arm's distance, try to make contact. If you're apart, think of a creative way to reach out and touch the one you love. Leave a message on his voice mail, fax her a love note, e-mail him a message that is filled with symbols and word pictures that only the two of you will understand. Surprise your sweetheart—stop by home or his or her office just to whisper, "I love you," then drop a single rose on his or her desk as you leave. Or call your loved one and read a few verses of poetry over the phone.

Romantic moments need not take a lot of money, just a little bit of time spent thinking about the one you love. After all, the gift your lover most enjoys is you!

> *Love is not getting, but giving.*
>
> HENRY VAN DYKE

Remind yourself of each other even when you're not together. I like to give Bill a quick "I love you" call in the midst of a hectic work day. When changing my clothes, I might pull his suit from the closet just to smell the fragrance of his cologne. I keep romantic cards he's given me close by so I can read them time and again. But my favorite way to prepare my heart to enjoy Bill is to take a quiet minute alone in the car or at my desk, close my eyes, and reflect upon one of our special, intimate moments together. I set aside my daily distractions and focus my thoughts on him, and it draws my heart close to his.

I keep many pictures of Pam in my office. I call home regularly throughout the day—sometimes just to hear her voice on the answering machine! I close my eyes and remember romantic times together. I periodically like to go shopping for her. Buying her something romantic or beautiful keeps my heart longing to be with her. And I keep a list of things that I can do for Pam with me at all times.

❧ MAKE A LIST—CHECK IT TWICE ❧

Discover what is romantic to each of you. Try these exercises:

Why Valentine's Day?

The legend of St. Valentine dates back to early Rome. Each year, the Romans celebrated a holiday in honor of their god, Lupercus. It became a festival for lovers. On February 15, they also worshiped Juno, the goddess of marriage. On this festival day, the young women would drop their names into a jar so young men could draw them out. They would then be partners for the holiday. But not everyone in Rome worshiped the legendary gods. Some Christians, who worshiped their one true God, also lived in the city under heavy persecution.

In 496, Pope Gelasius wished to commemorate the Christian view of true love. He looked for a martyr who had exhibited a life of loving others. He came across the story of St. Valentine. There are two legends of St. Valentine (this might be because Valentine was a common name at the time). One is that St. Valentine was a Christian doctor. He lived to help other people get well. He would even pray for his patients after he had given them medicine. St. Valentine was also a local Christian leader.

In those days it was illegal for Roman soldiers to marry. Claudius "The Cruel" wanted all men to go to war, so he did not allow them to marry. St. Valentine felt for these young people in love and would perform secret wedding ceremonies. When Claudius discovered St. Valentine, he had him jailed.

While in jail, St. Valentine met the jailer's daughter, a young blind girl. In Rome during this era, the blind were seen as cursed—unlovable—but St. Valentine befriended her and treated her blindness. (In the second legend about St. Valentine and the blind girl, some accounts say that he may have known her previously and treated her blindness with salve, hoping it would help her regain her sight—and this too angered the Roman authorities.) St. Valentine was sentenced to die on February 14. It was said that he wrote a note of encouragement to the jailor's daughter and signed it, "from your Valentine." Legend says that when the jailer's daughter unrolled the papyrus note from Valentine, for the first time in her life she could see!

Whatever you do,
do it with love!
The Book of 1 Corinthians

Spend time individually making a list of ten free things that you'd like your loved one to do for you. Some things might be obvious: Say "I love you," "Give me a hug," or "Hold my hand." Some things might not be so obvious: "Help me fold the clothes," "Make me dessert after I've cooked dinner," or "Surprise me by mowing the lawn." Make a date to exchange lists and talk about why you placed each item on the list. That's where you'll discover deeper insight about what is romantic to the one you love. And that romance can evolve.

For example, since we've married, on my list is "Run a bubble bath for me, light some candles, then come sit and talk with me, maybe even massage my back." This way I am assured of Bill's undivided attention as I get a quiet, uninterrupted moment away from my hectic schedule. When we were dating, my list included things like: Come visit me at work, go on a walk together, or take me to the beach at sunset.

You can also make a list of "Dream Dates." If money were no object, what ten dates would each of you like to go on during the year? You will get some wonderful birthday or anniversary ideas out of this one. Maybe you can't afford Hawaii this year—but you *can* afford island music, passion fruit, guava juice, and theater tickets to "South Pacific." Again, ask the one you love why these dates sound so romantic to him or her. You'll discover more about your loved one as your hearts grow closer.

Create Anticipation: Send roses to your sweetheart along with a note saying how anxious you are to see her. Call him on the phone and leave a message on his voice mail telling him how much you long to be with him. (Be sure that it is voice mail for his ears only!) Send each other a card each day for a month, two weeks, or one week prior to a much-anticipated vacation or anniversary.

> *All our actions take hue*
> *from the complexion of the heart.*
>
> FRANCIS BACON

Buy a new outfit, spicy cologne, or fragrant perfume. Or, better yet, wrap up one of these items and deliver it to your loved one with a note that proclaims your desperate yearning to be with him or her.

Create a Plan: Prepare for your special date or getaway. Plan ahead and pack things that will make life easier once you get there. For example, call ahead to the bed and breakfast that you are staying at and check to see if they pack picnic baskets for guests, or if they'll supply the basket and you need to bring the sandwiches and sparkling cider.

Small touches really count! If you go on a midnight outing to the beach for a campfire and a snuggle under the moonlight, bring a warm wool blanket or sleeping bags, firewood, matches, and kindling or newspaper. You'll most likely remember your guitar or a tape player and cassette, but don't forget towels to dry yourselves off in case you decide to go wading.

Even if your special date is at home, you can plan ahead to create a romantic mood. Think of the route that your loved one will walk as he or she enters the house. Place a love

Romantic Fireside Picnic for Two

If your heart is longing for a picnic but rain or snow is falling outside, don't despair! You can still keep warm and dry and have a cozy picnic with the one you love. Light a fire in the fireplace and get ready for an evening filled with the warmth of romance! You'll need—

- hot dogs, buns, and condiments

- old-fashioned potato salad

- colorful paper plates and plasticware

- sparkling cider or other fancy chilled beverage and glasses

- mocha truffles

- marshmallows, chocolate bars, and graham crackers—for S'mores!

- thermos of your favorite coffee and mugs

After you've lit the fire, place soft blankets and cozy pillows on the floor. You can even wrap up together in a toasty blanket! Create skewers out of metal clothes *hangers and roast hot dogs in the fireplace. Serve each other sparkling cider, which can be decorated with your own private label! See who can make the perfect S'more, then hold each other, sip coffee, and talk as the firelight flickers and dances.*

MOCHA TRUFFLES

2 packages (12 oz.) semi-sweet chocolate chips

1 package (8 oz.) softened cream cheese

3 Tbsp. instant coffee granules

2 tsp. water

1 lb. dark chocolate confectionery coating

In a microwave-safe bowl, melt chocolate chips. Add cream cheese, coffee, and water; mix well. Chill until firm enough to shape. Shape into 1-inch balls and place on waxed paper-lined cookie sheet. Chill 1 to 2 hours or until firm. Melt chocolate coating in microwave. Dip balls and place on waxed paper to harden.

Yields 5 ½ dozen.

note or small gift on the front doorstep, sprinkle a path of con-
fetti hearts or fragrant rose petals to create an enchanting
walkway to the dining room. You can also create a lighted path
by using luminaries (bags filled with sand and votive candles),
candles, or balloons. Use your imagination! A variation of this
theme is to place notes containing clues that, one by one, lead
your lover to you, to a gift, or to an unexpected romantic
adventure—like dinner on the rooftop.

Ask each other heart-to-heart questions, or choose a
favorite poem to read aloud. Better yet, write your own poetry.

Create a Sensory Experience: Using your five senses, prepare
a romantic setting.

Smells So Good! How can you make your home smell
beautiful? Try scented candles, potpourri in a bowl, fresh flowers, scent rings on light bulbs, or potpourri burners. Another
great smell is that of delicious food. Bake a batch of cookies, a
loaf of fresh bread, a pan of brownies, or cook a gourmet meal!
You can also make yourself smell terrific. When we visited the
Hawaiian Islands, we stocked up on cocoa butter tanning
sticks—just because we love the smell!

Looks So Good! Scan your surroundings. Are they clean?
Things don't have to be perfect—just cozy and comfortable.
Rooms always feel warmer in soft lighting. Decorate a room
with candles, invest in sconces for your walls, or place a hurricane
lamp on the dresser. Tiny white Christmas lights give an elegant
feel to any setting. Weave a few strands of lights on a tree, or
string them on your ceiling to create that "starry night" effect.

In the daylight, plants and fresh flowers go a long way in creating a romantic setting, as do piles of pillows or fresh white linen topped with china and crystal. If you can't create the setting, travel to a romantic setting like a lakeside cabin, beach cottage, mountain resort, a charming garden, or a fine restaurant for at least part of the date.

Tastes So Good! Try a variety of palate pleasers. Set out a bowl of fresh strawberries, fine chocolates, or a plate of petit fours. It always works well to include something you know your sweetheart adores.

If I want to cheer Pam up, I'm sure to please her heart by ordering her some Dewar's Chews—a tasty taffy from Pam's hometown in Bakersfield, California. By having some chews on hand, I let her know that I have been thinking of her. She's always impressed because I had to take an extra step and order them!

Sounds So Good! Invest in romantic music that both of you love. If your musical tastes are different, try something new to both of you. For example, if she loves country music and you love rock and roll, then try some jazz or classical music playing very softly in the background. Or listen to music from the Caribbean, Africa, or South America!

Another wonderful option is romantic music with a positive message. Look for lyrics that promote commitment, sacrifice, and sensitivity. Let the lyrics encourage your relationship as you relax together. These songs are a welcome break from the less-positive lyrics of many country or pop songs.

The Perfect Outdoor Picnic

Plan ahead for a romantic afternoon or evening picnic with your sweetheart.

• A cozy blanket and a plastic tablecloth (lay plastic side down on the ground to keep out moisture and to protect the blanket).

• Food that is easy to handle: cheese and crackers, deli meats, a bottle of shrimp cocktail, a French bread baguette, sliced fresh fruit, vegetables with dip, and cookies or chocolates. Don't forget the dill pickles!

• Sparkling grape juice or cider (chilled) and festive glasses.

• Quality plasticware—or even colorful paper plates. Real china is terrific, as are cloth napkins. To protect china and crystal, wrap them carefully in a towel. You can also use the towel for cleanup!

- *A book of poetry, some of your favorite love notes, or a sketchbook for journaling thoughts and drawing pictures together.*

- *Fragrant candles, pretty candlesticks, and matches.*

- *A small jar filled with water to hold a centerpiece of fresh flowers. Bring a bouquet or pick some wildflowers!*

- *Romantic music. It is a real treat if you play the guitar or flute! But a radio or CD player will work just fine.*

- *A map—nothing spoils the mood faster than an argument over whether you are lost or not!*

- *Sunscreen and sunglasses for warm weather; a sweater and gloves for a cooler day.*

- *Bug spray (keep in a separate container away from the food). Keep away the ants and mosquitoes!*

- *Water and a first-aid kit, especially if you're hiking to your picnic destination.*

Feels So Good! Consider what might feel nice next to your skin. Favorite romantic settings often include the ocean, a Jacuzzi, or a swimming pool. Incorporate massage, lotion, satin, silk, or velvet into your times together. We often wear clothes because they feel good next to our skin, but consider how the fabric feels on the outside. Bill has some sweaters that feel scratchy and itchy to me, while others are soft and invite me into his arms.

Think of creative ways to enhance your romance. You'll stay heart to heart.

Love not the gift but the giver.

WILLIAM SHAKESPEARE

FREE (OR NEARLY FREE) GREAT DATES

Romance doesn't have to cost money to be great. The best romantic moments are often free or nearly free because they usually are accompanied by lots of love and creativity! These free or nearly free ideas will make your dates together a pure pleasure.

• *Have a candlelight picnic in an unusual location— up on your rooftop, sitting on a park bench, or relaxing on a blanket with a view of the ocean.*

• *Go on a photo date where you snap photos of each other all over the city. If finances allow, take the film to a one-hour developer. Frame your favorite shot and give it to your spouse with a love note. The other photos can be sent as postcards to each other all year long.*

• *Walk or bicycle (tandem bike if you have access to one!) to an old-fashioned ice cream shop or a cozy coffeehouse.*

• *Drive to the mountains, arriving in time for a sunset or moonlit stroll.*

- Go to a park, swing together, and talk. Take turns listing—A to Z—the reasons you love each other.

- Walk the mall. Your goal is not to buy, but to find a perfect perfume and cologne. Test as many as you can, then people watch!

- Have a squirt-gun fight. If it's really hot, run through a sprinkler or turn on the hose!

- Write clues on dime-store Valentines and place them around town, then take your love on a car rally or treasure hunt. The date consists of gathering clues and small romantic treasures like poems, chocolates, and other tiny treats.

- Go to the library and check out a poetry book or a romantic classic novel. Read the book together.

- Write a song or poem and read it to the one you love. Even an original version of "Roses Are Red" can be a treasure since it's from the heart.

- Reenact a portion of great romantic drama. Shakespeare's Romeo and Juliet is a wonderful place to begin.

- *Reminisce over old photo albums or your wedding album. Set the mood by relaxing together by firelight or candlelight. Another option is to have your children or friends play waiter and waitress and serve you a romantic dinner. Be sure to leave a tip!*

- *Buy an encouraging book on relationships, and read it together.*

- *Have a living-room luau. Play island music.*

- *Borrow plants from your friends and neighbors and turn your patio into a private garden retreat. Enjoy a quiet dinner and classical music.*

- *Rent a nostalgic, romantic movie. Films from the '30s to '50s are a good place to start. Current movies are often remakes of older films. The original is often more romantic.*

- *Search through the kids' toy chest. Go fly a kite at the park or play some one-on-one basketball.*

- *Work out together. Go for a jog, take a long bike ride, or play racquetball at the gym.*

- Bake something extravagant together. Bonus points if you both help clean up!

- Play a board game together. Classics like Scrabble or the Ungame are good conversation starters. Or show your competitive side at Monopoly.

- Put on your special song and waltz around the living room, or find some new romantic music.

- Play twenty questions. Each of you think of ten questions you'd love to know the answer to, such as, "If you introduced me to someone I didn't know, what one thing would you say that you really appreciate about me?" or "If money was not a factor, where would you like to go on a romantic getaway?"

- Go to a church or a beautiful spot outdoors. Take turns praying and thanking God for one another.

- Buy a box of jelly beans. Take turns feeding them to each other. Don't look at the jelly beans as you eat them—try to guess the flavor!

- *Go berry picking together. Stop at a 25-cent lemonade stand on the way home.*

- *Recycle all your aluminum cans and bottles. Use the money to buy a small treat or dessert at your favorite restaurant.*

- *Wait for the ice cream truck on a hot summer day. Choose treats for each other.*

- *Go to a free concert in a park or listen to a street musician. Dance!*

- *Take a midnight dip in a lake, ocean, or hot tub.*

- *Go horseback riding—on the same horse.*

- *Lie back in the grass and gaze at the stars.*

Remember, it's not the expense of the gift, but the thought that counts!

CHAPTER 5

Romancing the Heart

GREAT GETAWAYS

*Knit your hearts with
an unslipping knot.*

WILLIAM SHAKESPEARE

"THE BAHAMAS?"

"I'd love to go, but we don't have that kind of money."

"Hawaii?"

"Get serious!"

"I am! I want to go somewhere exotic! Somewhere new
and far away."

"Okay, I've got it! How about the mountains? The
Rockies? Jackson Hole, Wyoming? Montana?"

"In a cozy cabin. By a roaring fire. Peace and quiet.

Deep in the forest. Yeah, I could get into that."

"It has to be by a lake."

"Yes, a vacation by water just seems more relaxing—"

"And romantic."

"Anywhere with you—alone—will be romantic!"

Alone. Lovers love to be there—together. Just the two of you. Quiet days, quiet meals, long walks, and deep talks. By stepping away from the daily routine, you gain time to fall in love all over again. Often couples think that the family vacation should be enough, but traveling with children or other adults doesn't give you the cozy, intimate time that you and your loved one need.

There are many outstanding types of getaways for lovers. Maybe one of these will inspire you to escape this weekend!

The R and R Getaway: Time off for rest and relaxation. Time to do absolutely nothing. Lie in the sun, read novels, recreate, and slow down. Couples who live a fully packed, fast-paced life are wise to give themselves these times on a regular basis. We can return to our daily lives happier and healthier after a quiet, isolated getaway. Bill and I aim at having a twenty-four hour oasis quarterly, when we can temporarily leave our schedules and agendas behind. Be spontaneous—pack a toothbrush, some lingerie, a bathing suit, and head out! Let your whims carry you.

•Try flipping a coin to decide where to go—left or right, north or south.

CHOCOLATE "LET'S GET COZY" FONDUE

Note: If you drop something off the fondue fork and into the main pot, tradition says you owe your lover a kiss!

> 1 15-oz. can sweetened condensed milk
>
> 1 pint jar of marshmallow creme
>
> 1 6-oz. package of semi-sweet chocolate chips
>
> (Optional: $\frac{1}{3}$ c. crushed butter mints or a mint-chocolate candy bar)
>
> $\frac{1}{4}$ c. milk
>
> (Optional: 2 Tbsp. creme de cocoa)

In a saucepan, combine and melt. Keep warm in a fondue pot. Cut up bananas, angel food or pound cake, or use whole maraschino cherries, strawberries, or mandarin orange sections. Dip and feed to the one you love. Take your time!

• Choose a city you've never visited, or one you'd like to explore more of. Go to the tourist bureau or Chamber of Commerce to discover unique economical accommodations.

• Pretend to kidnap your sweetheart. Call ahead and book appointments under a false name. Coordinate with his or her secretary, then walk in with a blindfold and steal your love away to a surprise location. You'll need to plan—but your loved one will be thrilled with the "unplan."

• Leave your watches at home. Sleep when you're tired and eat when you're hungry. Play.

• Get away on an off day. Often mid-week accommodations are less expensive in tourist towns, and weekend rates can be less expensive at downtown hotels that cater to business clientele.

A Planning Getaway. Once a year, Bill and I set aside a special time away to talk over the business side of our lives. We set goals, talk finances, plan for the children's needs, and match calendars and do scheduling for the year. This valuable time away is when we discuss and evaluate our expectations. We talk over career plans, business items, pace of life—anything that either of us sees as a challenge to be overcome. By taking these regular planning getaways, we keep our anniversary and birthday getaways free from distractions—and then we can really enjoy each other rather than have the mood ruined by discussions about work or finances.

You have stolen my heart . . .

THE SONG OF SONGS

To get the most relaxation and direction out of your planning getaway, try these helpful hints:

Set a Date, Then Delegate: Share the responsibility for making reservations, child-care or housesitting arrangements, and any other details. Decide who will do what. Get your trip off to a smooth start.

Play First: Plan a fun activity, a nap, and a good meal all before you begin setting goals or making decisions. You'll feel relaxed, refreshed, and ready to accomplish a lot.

Put First Things First: Remind yourself of your life priorities. If you've never written a mission statement for your relationship, start there. Write down the values and priorities that are important to both of you. Write down your goals and dreams. Having a plan for your relationship will build trust and confidence!

The Surprise Getaway. This is a sure way to keep the spontaneity in a relationship. We "plan" our surprises. For example, on each other's birthdays we plan a surprise that's creative and out of the ordinary. Take turns planning your getaways so that one of you is always surprised. These take a lot of preparation on the part of the one doing the "whisking" and a lot of flexibility on the part of the one being "whisked." And they're exciting for both of you!

The Un-Getaway. This can be the most creative as well as the easiest to do. These are those quick overnighters when the kids or pets go to grandma's or to a friend's and you transform your place into an instant retreat. This getaway takes little money or

A Great Getaway and a Full Piggy Bank!

- Book far in advance. Airlines offer substantial savings for those who plan ahead.

- Request the same rate that you paid previously—or ask for the same rate a friend paid. One couple heard that a nice hotel room, with breakfast included, was only $17 a night for their friends. When they called, they mentioned this special and the hotel honored that rate.

- Check in with the tourist bureau. Often hotels will call in a "sale" on rooms about mid-morning in order to fill up the rooms. You can get a great room for a great price!

- Swap homes with friends for a weekend. We once traded our Los Angeles apartment for our friends' home in the suburbs. They loved our pool and we loved their quiet neighborhood.

- *Go camping! Some camping resorts offer cozy, fully furnished cabins. Or backpack—the wilderness is beautiful and private.*

- *Try private conference facilities—especially during the week. These conference grounds usually cater to weekend camps so they may have rooms or cabins available during the week for nearly nothing.*

- *After you arrive in a city, check out the local library or coffeehouse for free magazines or newspapers that offer food and hotel specials to locals. Be on the lookout for free entertainment as well!*

- *Go on a twenty-four-hour getaway to a place you'd like to stay longer. While you are there, collect tourist brochures and information. Look for deals to take advantage of when you return for a long vacation!*

planning. You can curl up together on the sofa and watch a romantic movie, have a picnic in the backyard under the stars, or give each other massages. These instant retreats can be a welcome relief for busy couples!

1. Make It Different. Turn your home into a cozy bed and breakfast by stringing twinkling tiny white Christmas lights around your ceiling—it's a starlight atmosphere with more privacy. Or buy all the foods you never usually eat—chocolate mousse, gourmet potato chips, imported candies. Go with a theme—borrow plants and turn your patio into a Hawaiian paradise.

2. Make It Private. Leave the kids or pets with friends, grandparents, or relatives. Unplug technology—turn off the phones, pagers, fax machines. Park cars in the garage—or down the block so it doesn't look like you're home. Put a note on your front door instructing people to come back after a certain time. One couple even hung a "Quarantined" sign in their window!

3. Make It Personal. Write a poem, pull out photo albums, listen to a new CD, or plan a quiet movie or game that is your loved one's favorite! Each of you can plan a personal touch beforehand. Rent her favorite video. Wear his favorite nightie. Make the time uniquely yours.

The Building Getaway. This is for relationship tune-ups and enrichment. We recommend that couples go to a workshop or conference once a year. If you build into your love life before the crisis hits, you'll find that no crisis can tear you apart! You can also plan your own relationship-strengthening weekend where you read a book together, do an inspirational study, or watch or listen to encouraging videos or audiotapes. The key to a healthy relationship-building getaway is to choose positive input that values your commitment and uniqueness. Come together to renew your spiritual, emotional, and physical life—and your love!

Plan a time away soon—just the two of you. Let your hearts connect as you discover each other in a new or surprise location.

> *Love is an irresistible desire to be irresistibly desired.*
>
> ROBERT FROST

CREATE YOUR OWN HOLIDAY

Look for unique reasons to celebrate together!
Try these creative anniversaries:

The date you first kissed. *Celebrate by finding a great new place to kiss. Take a drive or visit the library to find unexplored romantic spots near you.*

The date you met. *Go back and celebrate at the place you met, or go somewhere that celebrates another era—a '50s diner, a '60s coffeehouse, or a '70s disco. Dress up for the occasion!*

The date you got engaged. *Celebrate by returning to where you honeymooned—or where you wish you had had enough money to honeymoon. Another option is to visit a glamour-type photo studio, then set a date to exchange those sensual shots.*

The birthdays of your children. *Send each other thank-you cards. Include photos of both of you with your children.*

The day you finally got out of debt. *Look for the most romantic idea you can do on $5!*

THE AFFAIR

It began as a surprise. Over dinner one night, he said he had to go to a convention for work. My heart sank. Away again, I thought. I already missed him. "It's only a few days," he said, stroking my hair reassuringly. I nodded and said, "It's just that we get so little time alone."

The next morning, after he'd left for work, I called his office and found out the name of the hotel where he would be staying during the convention. Then I called and arranged for a friend to come stay with the kids.

The day rushed by in a flurry. I packed a picnic basket with candles, chocolate, two glasses, and a bottle of sparkling cider tied with a big bow. The bow covered the tiny thing I packed to wear later that night. I grabbed a portable stereo and a new soft jazz cassette. I added my makeup bag and a toothbrush to my suitcase.

On the way out of town, I stopped at the mall. *A new outfit. A night like this needs a new outfit. Something he'll remember. After looking through several stores, I found it—a long azul sweater with tight black leggings—the perfect outfit!*

Back in the car, I listened to love songs on the radio—songs we'd danced to, sang to each other in whispered tones under soft lights. I felt my heart was being drawn to him. The lights from the oncoming cars on the freeway danced and flickered. Tonight was going to be special—a secret rendezvous, a liaison. My heart raced as the car sped me toward my destination. I imagined lying quietly in his arms, resting my head on his chest. I breathed deeply and could almost smell the deliciously familiar fragrance of his aftershave.

Parking the car discreetly behind a nearby business, I looked at my watch and sighed in relief. I had timed

*it just right. He would still be at the banquet, so
I had time to sneak into his room undetected.*

*I must have seemed a little flustered when I asked
for his room number and key because the desk clerk
replied, "I'm sorry, ma'am, we only have one person
registered for that room." A little panicked, I pulled
myself together and answered as confidently as I could,
"I'm his wife, and he wasn't sure if I'd be able to
get off work to come." He nodded his head and
handed me the key.*

*I quickly walked across the parking lot, my arms full
of the treasures of a woman in love, my heart filled
with anticipation. Again, I glanced at my watch.*
I'll have to hurry to get everything set up.
I want the atmosphere just perfect when he
steps into the room.

And it was perfect. Soft, flickering candlelight
danced across the ceiling to the mellow sound of the
smooth saxophone as he stepped into the room.
He stared at me in stunned amazement. As I ran
to him, he wrapped his arms around me, twirled me
around, and whispered, "Wow! What a surprise.
I'm so glad you've come." Then we kissed, danced,
and finally fell asleep in each other's arms.
It all felt so good—so right—as I could hear
the beat of his heart.

The quiet beeping of my alarm clock pulled me
from my dreams the next morning. Why can't
these moments last forever? I thought, quietly
slipping into my clothes and gathering up the
tokens of romance I had brought with me.
I ran my fingers through his hair and we kissed.
He thanked me again for coming

*and smiled his special smile. As I drove
out of the parking lot, the sun was peeking up from
its slumber and a ray of sunlight spilled across the
steering wheel. It sparkled on my diamond ring—
the ring my husband had given me fifteen years
earlier. I smiled. An affair to remember—an affair
with my beloved husband.*

Whatever our souls are made of,
his and mine are the same.

Emily Brontë

CHAPTER 6

Winning Hearts

WHEN LIFE GETS YOU DOWN, LOVE CAN LIFT YOU UP

*A gentle heart is tied
with an easy thread.*

GEORGE HERBERT

"I NOW PRONOUNCE YOU HUSBAND AND WIFE. You may kiss the bride."

After the kiss, you clasp hands and hurry down the aisle, feeling like a million bucks! But can love really conquer all when reality hits? When it rains on your parade or you're looking for that silver lining in the storm cloud that just hit, love can lift you higher. When the demands of life—children, career, volunteer work, family, and friends—put pressure on us, Bill and I have committed to not blaming each other. Instead, we look at each other and say, "It's not you. It's not me. It's just

SACRIFICE OR PRIVILEGE?

*". . . if I ever did a good deed in my life—if ever
I thought a good thought—if ever I prayed a sincere
and blameless prayer—if ever I wished a righteous
wish—I am rewarded now. To be your wife is, for me,
to be as happy as I can be on earth."*

"Because you delight in sacrifice."

*"Sacrifice! What do I sacrifice? Famine for food,
expectation for content. To be privileged to put my arms
round what I value—to press my lips to what I love—
to repose on what I trust: is that to make sacrifice?
If so, then certainly I delight in sacrifice."*

CHARLOTTE BRONTË
Jane Eyre

life." This is our way of saying "We're teammates. We can get through anything together!" When your hearts are intertwined, love can conquer all!

❧ LOVE THAT GOES THE DISTANCE ❧

The car wasn't gorgeous, but it ran. That is, it ran until the day that steam poured from the engine and the car sadly chugged to the side of the road. Bill had returned to school with two quarters of schooling left. Together, we held three part-time jobs that didn't equal one full-time income, so there was no money for a new car or a new engine. For the next six months we rode our bikes everywhere. We rode together in fog so dense that we couldn't see much more than a bike's length ahead. Day after day, riding those bikes forged our hearts together. Every day Bill thanked me for my willingness to sacrifice for his education.

As the spring progressed and the weather warmed, I became excited. Now we'd *finally* have some money—a real job, my turn for my dreams, either having children or finishing my degree. Then reality hit again—Bill received a partial scholarship for graduate school. Again, I set aside my own dreams to work to help Bill finish his graduate degree. Four years later when Bill got his M. Div., he bought me a beautiful new dress, took me out to dinner, lavished me with roses, and handed me a tiny gift-wrapped box. Inside was a class ring from his school with the initials "P.H.T." engraved on the side. He said I deserved recognition for his degree as much as he did, so he presented me with a thank-you ring for "Putting Hubby Through." I felt like a winner!

❈ I'M ON YOUR TEAM! ❈

I was very excited when Bill shared with me his dream of wanting to be a senior pastor. We had helped build a thriving youth ministry in a large church, but we were both sensing that we needed a change.

I was an optimistic cheerleader through all the days of resumes and interviews. When Bill was finally offered a position as senior pastor of a church near San Diego, I was elated—until we moved from our three-bedroom home into a tiny apartment. After we moved in, the manager informed us that our two energetic preschool boys were not allowed to play on the grass, nor could they ride their tricycles on the sidewalk. I'd given up a nice house, great friends, and a satisfying leadership role for this lifestyle? Over the next few weeks, depression hit me like a tidal wave. I was struggling with who I was, what my new role would be in this church and community, and how I would survive such a drastic change.

One day I went to the closet to get a box off the top shelf. As I reached for it, everything fell off the shelf and scattered across the floor. The next thing I knew, I was sitting and sobbing on top a load of dirty laundry.

"Mommy, what's wrong?" asked my two little boys.

"I don't know," I moaned.

I gathered the boys onto my lap, rocked them, and prayed. Then I realized something. I knew that Bill cared about me and that our family was more important than his job. I needed

Love Is Saying "I'm Sorry."

Say It Big: If you've had an ongoing argument or if you really put your foot in your mouth, try saying "I'm sorry" in just as big a way as you blew it. Hang a sign made from a sheet over a freeway overpass, bake a huge, heart-shaped cookie and write "I'm sorry" on it, or fill a room with balloons, each with an apology tied to it.

Say It Face-to-Face: It's wonderful to receive a card or a note, but nothing will strengthen a relationship more than a face-to-face meeting. Catch up with the one you love (wherever he or she is—work, school, home) and walk up to him or her and say, "I'm sorry. I was wrong." Give your loved one a hug and a kiss.

Say It Uniquely: Leave a small gift (perfume, a chocolate treat, jewelry, or tickets for a future date) in a place where your sweetheart will be sure to find it (taped to the car's steering wheel, on the pillow or mirror, or on his or her desk at work). Try cutting out a picture of a foot and a face—and say you're sorry and you put your foot in your mouth. Leave the note with a bouquet of flowers on the front door.

Say It Over and Over: Send a card, a small gift, or a single rose with a note each hour all day—or once a day for several days. Word the apology in different ways: "I'm sorry; I was wrong; I was mistaken; I am fallible; Please forgive me." Try to explain what was going on in your mind, what you learned about yourself from the situation, or what you value about your sweetheart since the disagreement. See the misunderstanding as an opportunity to gain greater insight and intimacy.

Say It with Sentiment: Write a poem with pen and paper or try magnetic poetry, a set of words that can be arranged into poems on your refrigerator. Quote an apology from your sweetheart's favorite book or movie, or create a gift that captures your humble heart—a song, a painting, or a story.

Love is an act of endless forgiveness.

PETER USTINOV

to find a way to encourage him and let him know what I was feeling. I needed to support him—with love, honesty, and kindness.

A few days later, I called Bill at work and invited him out to lunch. Over lunch, I reached across the table and took his hand. "I'm sorry for the way I have treated you. I just want you to know that I'm on your team. I'm here to support and encourage you."

Bill breathed a huge sigh of relief. Over the next few months, I saw his enthusiasm for life return—and my happiness come back. And I've learned one thing for sure: Working with Bill as a teammate sure beats sitting on a pile of dirty laundry any day!

❧ CHEERING TO THE FINISH LINE ❧

It's not always easy being teammates. Pam and I had many long discussions about her desire to spread her wings. She wanted to return to school and pursue a writing career. We had a plan, but she wanted to jump ahead of schedule. We still had children at home, and Pam was a great mom, wife, lover, and friend. But her desire to fulfill her dreams put pressure on me to help share the household duties even more. And I liked our life as it was!

After much thought and prayer, I finally came to the point where I could encourage Pam in her pursuits. I wanted to show her how completely I now supported her. One day I had to be on Pam's campus for a church project. Pam would be in class that day and before she left for school, she said, "Think of me when you are at school today." That's when I got a terrific idea.

Pam was in a medieval literature class that morning. The professor, leaning against the chalkboard, had just announced that romance was dead. He pointed out that romance was an idealistic fallacy in the Middle Ages and simply unobtainable today. Many women in the room nodded in agreement.

In the middle of this diatribe on the state of men in our world, I walked into the room. I made my way over to Pam's desk, which was inconveniently located in the middle of the room. I placed a dozen red roses in her arms, bent down over her shoulder, and whispered, "I love you." I then gave her a kiss and left the room as quickly as I had come in.

"Is it your birthday?" the startled professor asked Pam.

"No."

"Your anniversary?"

"No."

"Then why did he bring you roses?"

"I guess he just wanted me to know that he loves me and believes in me!"

Then many of the women in the class asked, "Does he have a brother?"

I had struggled with Pam in a big way as she tried to pursue her dream. I wanted her to know, in an even bigger way, that I now believed in her and her dream!

There are many fine women in the world,
but you are the best of them all!

THE BOOK OF PROVERBS

❧ THE EQUALITY OF TRUE LOVE ❧

One romantic, meaningful activity to enjoy together is to take a look back. What were those anchor points in your love? For me, my heart will never forget that Bill built a home for me. He didn't have it built; he built it with his own hands, his own sweat, and, at times, his own tears. A part of Bill's heart is in each room. I know only his deep, committed love for me kept him going on nights when it was cold and rainy. Thinking of his love and sacrifice warms my heart.

I am also eternally grateful that Bill believed in me and my dream to write. When I returned to finish my degree, it was not easy for Bill. He first believed in my dream by faith—knowing it was right. Then he allowed his heart to catch up and, on my graduation day, he invited my friends and family and threw me a surprise party, complete with a recreation hall full of colorful helium balloons and a drama of "This Is Your Life!"

I see Heaven's glories shine,
And faith shines equal.

EMILY BRONTË

Bill continues to lift me up when things get busy. This last Christmas season, my calendar was filled with speaking engagement after speaking engagement. I knew he missed me as much as I was missing him when he dropped a small wrapped gift of makeup into my speaking bag. For the next fourteen days, I received a gift each day no matter where I found myself!

❁ LOVE FORGIVES AND ENCOURAGES ❁

In order to stay connected, Pete and Sandy made a decision not to spend more than two hundred dollars on anything without first consulting each other. They had kept this promise for about ten years when Sandy attended a small-business conference. She wanted to be home with her kids, but she also wanted to have a career. She thought that starting a home-based business could be the answer to her dreams.

As the seminar leader talked about the possibilities of a certain business opportunity, her heart was stirred. *I can do this*, Sandy thought. *In fact, I could be very good at this!*

Her thoughts were broken by the seminar leader, "If you sign up for this today, you can get started for five hundred dollars. If you wait, it will cost fifteen hundred dollars."

I know I'm not supposed to spend the money without consulting Pete, but this is such a great opportunity. I'm sure he will understand. And he'll be proud if I saved us a thousand dollars. So Sandy paid the five hundred dollars, confident that her new business would succeed.

When Sandy came home and walked in the door, she heard Pete working on the computer. She took a deep breath and headed for the den. "Pete," she said, "I'm going to tell you something and I need you to say, 'I believe in you, Sandy, and I'm confident you are going to make this work.'"

"Okay, Sandy. What is this all about?"

"I know I broke our agreement, but it was such a great opportunity! I went to a seminar and found a business opportunity that is perfect for me. I spent five hundred dollars today to open up a new business. I know I should have talked with you first, but they told us that it would cost fifteen hundred dollars after the seminar."

Pete took a deep breath. On the one hand, he was proud of Sandy for taking a step forward in her career. On the other hand, he felt betrayed for having not been consulted about the decision.

"Well, Sandy," he said, "I believe in you, and I think you can make this work."

Sandy gave Pete a big hug, thanked him for his support, and got right to work at making her business a success. She planned well, did her homework, and worked hard with confidence and creativity. But the business never got off the ground. It wasn't the perfect fit she thought it would be. Finally, she had to admit to Pete that her business was not working.

Tears were trickling down Sandy's cheeks as she cried out her heart to Pete. She had broken their agreement, and now she had failed.

Her heart came out of the shadows and into the sunshine when Pete said, "Let's just consider this the cost of your education. If you had gotten a master's degree, it would have cost much more! Let's just move on from here. You are talented, and you will be successful in many other areas. I love you, Sandy, and I want a wife who is happy."

Sandy lost that five hundred dollars, but she has gone on to run a very successful business. Now her husband often teases,

"I'll get to retire soon—or maybe I'll come work for you, Sandy!"

❀ LOVE IN THOSE DAILY IRRITATIONS ❀

For me, choosing to not expect Bill to make up for one of his key faults has brought freedom and grace to our love life. A month before our wedding, Bill and I went to our pastor for premarital counseling.

The pastor asked, "Pam, what is the one fault of Bill's that drives you crazy?"

I sat silent for a long while. I couldn't really think of any faults Bill had. Finally, I said, "Well, it's no big deal, but he's usually about seven minutes late."

The pastor smiled and said, "Well, if you can live with that, you'll be fine because it'll only get worse." And he was right. A few years into our marriage, I found that I was routinely frustrated with Bill for coming home late. One night I could hold back no longer. I told Bill how much his lateness bothered me, crying and pouring out my feelings. I went on and on. Then I glanced at the clock. An entire hour had passed. I was dismayed that I had lost thirty minutes with Bill because he'd come home late—and I was sadder that I had lost another hour with my complaining.

It was then that I remembered some advice from a doctor's wife: "Being married to an obstetrician, I never lose valuable time together complaining that he's not here enough."

That night I chose to forgive Bill—over and over—knowing that, because he works with people, he would probably be late on a regular basis. Bill is a great listener; people are a priority with him. That's why I fell in love with him.

Life is too short, and time is too precious to waste it holding a grudge.

*Do not let the sun go down
while you still are angry.*

THE BOOK OF EPHESIANS

❀ LOVE KNOWS NO BARRIERS ❀

On my grandparent's sixtieth wedding anniversary, we traveled back to Idaho to join in a huge celebration of friends and family. The morning of the party, Bill and I were sitting with my grandparents at the breakfast table. I said, "Well, Grandma and Grandpa, Bill and I travel all over the country giving marriage conferences. What advice should we give them? What's your secret? How did you make it sixty years together?"

They looked at one another, paused, then my grandmother tapped my grandfather's knee and said with a twinkle in her eye, "Pure grit and determination!"

Giving until the very end has its own priceless rewards. My grandmother had been ill for several years with a progressive failure of her respiratory system. My grandfather and grandmother had moved into my mother's home. Grandfather lovingly cared for grandmother, especially during the days while my mother worked. Often grandmother would wake him

Tokens of Love

*Hearts and flowers are sweet and always appreciated,
but sometimes it's fun to do something different. Try
borrowing a cherished custom from another time and
place to show your affection.*

A Handmade Gift

*Pennsylvania Dutch, Swiss, Scandinavian, and Welsh
peasants delighted in giving each other handmade love
tokens that were both sentimental and useful—cake
molds, butter prints, hand-carved wooden spoons, and
heart-shaped trinket boxes. Often, the lover inscribed a
message on the item for his or her beloved, such as:*

When this you see

Pray think of me

The many miles

We distant be

Altho' we are a great way apart

I wish you well with all my heart.

Take time to hand-make a gift for your loved one. He or she will cherish it always.

119

T.S. + F.J.

This custom is alive and well on school desks and in wet cement. The tradition of lovers linking their names or initials for all to see dates back to ancient Greece, when lovers carved their names together on trees.

Cherish every opportunity to connect your name with your beloved's—traced on a steamy window, written in frosting on a cake, or doodled on a piece of paper.

several times during the night because she felt she couldn't breathe. One night, she awakened my grandfather. "Gerald, could you hold me? I'm having a hard time breathing."

And this night, like so many others, he gathered the lover of his life into his arms. Gently he held her and rocked her into the arms of heaven. She breathed her last breath, knowing she was completely and totally loved.

Two persons must believe
in each other,
and feel that it can be done
and must be done;
in that way they are enormously strong.

VINCENT VAN GOGH

C H A P T E R 7

One Heart

DISCOVERING YOUR UNIQUE RELATIONSHIP

Romance is an attitude.
It is a man and woman being alive
to one another.

COLLEEN AND LOUIS EVANS, JR.

JUST WHAT IS ROMANCE? Is it flowers and candlelight? Unhurried time together? Cozy snuggling? Maybe. Is it a quiet walk on the beach or a leisurely stroll through the forest? Is it an adventurous date spent parasailing or scuba diving? Maybe. Is it a cup of espresso by the fire or sparkling cider on the dance floor? Is it red-and-black satin lingerie—or pristine white lace and cotton? Maybe. Romance is personal. Romance is all about each other's loves, likes, and preferences. That is why romance is unique to each couple.

24 Things to Always Remember . . . and One Thing to Never Forget

Your presence is a present to the world.
You're unique and one of a kind.
Your life can be what you want it to be.
Take the days just one at a time.

Count your blessings, not your troubles.
You'll make it through whatever comes along.
Within you are so many answers.
Understand, have courage, be strong.

Don't put limits on yourself.
So many dreams are waiting to be realized.
Decisions are too important to leave to chance.
Reach for your peak, your goal, your prize.

Nothing wastes more energy than worrying.
The longer one carries a problem,
the heavier it gets.
Don't take things too seriously.
Live a life of serenity, not a life of regrets.

Remember that a little love goes a long way.
Remember that a lot . . . goes forever.
Remember that friendship is a wise investment.
Life's treasures are people . . . together.

Realize that it's never too late.
Do ordinary things in an extraordinary way.
Have health and hope and happiness.
Take the time to wish upon a star.

And don't ever forget . . .
for even a day . . . how very special you are.

COLLIN McCARTY

It's only with time that true passion is built because it takes time to build trust. Get to know yourself and your partner intimately—and let him or her get to know you.

❈ CONNECTING HEART TO HEART ❈

I turned the key over in the ignition. Nothing. I tried it again. This time that all-too-familiar "click, click, click" was the only sound I could hear. Dead battery, maybe. Or perhaps a bad ignition connection. To keep my engine purring, I needed good connections.

Good connections. That's what love is all about. A connection between two hearts. And we can strengthen that by strengthening it strand by strand. When we built our home, I helped prepare the wiring for the electrical outlets and switches. In each electrical cable were strands of different colors. Each had to be prepared for a strong connection. In the same way, we need to carefully maintain each strand of our love for a strong connection between hearts.

❈ A PHYSICAL CONNECTION ❈

How you feel emotionally has a lot to do with the shape you're in physically. How is your health? How physically fit are you? What sports and activities can you enjoy with the one you love? How much sleep do you get? How well are you eating? View caring for your physical well-being, and the physical well-being of your loved one, as a way of caring for one strand of the connection.

A few years ago, Bill and I noticed that we had inadvertently allowed exercise to be squeezed out of our schedule.

Both of us grew up playing competitive sports. In our early years together, sports were a regular part of our dating life. As a New Year's resolution, we joined a fitness club that offered all the activities we enjoyed individually and some (like racquetball and a pool) that we could enjoy together. Now we have two standing workout dates a week. Sometimes, after our workout, we go out for a healthy breakfast where we have an opportunity to talk. We have found that we gain back that time and more. We feel stronger, have more energy, and get to spend fun time together!

Another great option for connecting on a physical level is to find a sport or activity that you enjoy as a couple. Or make a list of sports that neither of you are experts at or that you've always wanted to try—then try them! Bill and I bought in-line skates just to skate hand in hand by the beach together. You might enjoy ballroom dance lessons, tennis, or something completely out of the ordinary—like hang-gliding!

❧ AN INTELLECTUAL CONNECTION ❧

He may like reading, while you prefer hands-on experience. She may prefer lively conversation while you would rather enjoy a few quiet moments on the Internet. Or one of you may be learning a lot at work or school while the other is struggling to find time to learn anything new.

"He's in school and I'm at home with the baby. I feel like he's becoming an intellectual giant while my mind is becoming mush! Barney and microbiology don't have a lot in common. I'm afraid we're drifting apart."

"Love is patient, love is kind.
It does not envy, it does not boast,
it is not proud. It is not rude, it is not
self-seeking, it is not easily angered,
it keeps no record of wrongs.
Love does not delight in evil
but rejoices in the truth.
It always protects, always trusts,
always hopes, always perseveres.
Love never fails . . ."

THE BOOK OF 1 CORINTHIANS

Even if your interests and pursuits are different, you can build intellectual connections into your relationship.

• Become an appreciation professional. Even if you and the one you love have opposite interests, you can connect intellectually by appreciating the interests each other values most. Just by listening, you can connect with your loved one's heart.

• Connect by learning together. Take a class together just for fun. Make a list of things you've always wanted to learn about and a list of the most off-the-wall areas of interest you can think of. Either list them together in order of priority—or just draw from a hat! Then sign up for that class and have fun learning together.

• Try a common hobby. Look for a club that you can both join to explore a new interest, such as photography or sailing. Is there a cause you both believe in that you can do volunteer work for?

• Try reading together. You can read individually, then share what you are learning. Or you might try reading to one another.

❧ A SPIRITUAL CONNECTION ❧

Picture this: Adam and Eve in the garden of Eden. God announces, "and the two shall become one flesh." The connection is strengthened when there is a union made between a man and a woman with God as the anchor.

In the recent blockbuster movie hit *Twister*, there is a thrilling scene where the main characters go on the ride of their

BREAKFAST FOR THE YOUNG-AT-HEART

Breakfast dates are popular today—you and your sweetheart go out for some whole-wheat pancakes and fresh-squeezed orange juice. That kind of breakfast date is fun, healthy, and wholesome. But every once in a while you need to forget about calories and vitamins and return to your carefree childhood!

Get these preparations ready the night before—

•boxes of favorite childhood cereals for you and your lover—look for cereals with a surprise in the box!

•chocolate or strawberry milk

•your favorite juice or hot cocoa

•comfortable pajamas or sweats

•a small gift or toy

Linger over your breakfast, read the paper (starting with the comics!), and watch cartoons or reruns of favorite sitcoms from your childhood. Talk about your favorite childhood memories. You can even write each other love notes with invisible ink!

lives. The two scientists are chasing a tornado when the tornado suddenly turns toward them! Seeking lifesaving shelter, the two dart into a watershed. There, the man spots pipes that go at least thirty feet into the ground. He frantically suggests they strap themselves together, then strap themselves to the pipes. They do this just in time for the tornado to settle upon the shed. The shed gets pulverized around them as the two are lifted off the ground. They stare right into the eye of the tornado—yet they survive. They were strapped to the anchor—the pipes that held them safely in the midst of the twister. That is a picture of what knowing God personally can do for a couple in love. God can be a sure anchor, a protection for your love— no matter what twister life may send your way God can and will hold you heart to heart.

❄ A SOCIAL CONNECTION ❄

It's Thursday night. My heart races as I put on my makeup and change into a favorite outfit. My heart is beating fast. My face is flushed with excitement. I look at my watch. *He'll be here any minute.* It's date night—after 17 years, I still look forward to being with Bill. Date nights are one of the reasons.

*My love for you . . . is so deep and tender
that it seems to be outside myself.*

KATHERINE MANSFIELD

When we are teens, life revolves around the thrill and excitement of Friday and Saturday nights. As adults, too often we set aside having fun together because responsibilities pile up in our lives. But keeping date night a special night keeps the spark alive. Connecting on a social level will build an atmosphere where love can flourish. Planning is the wind beneath the wings of spontaneity, which keeps your hearts connected in a fast-paced world.

❃ FIVE IMPORTANT MINUTES ❃

Perhaps it's difficult to find that "quality time" together. Don't let a busy schedule pull your hearts apart. Use those five-minute bits of time to stay connected. When your schedule is ready for some quantity time, your hearts will be ready also. Take the little moments to stay heart to heart.

Give a Compliment. Bill routinely gives me compliments as a response to our everyday conversation. When I stop by his office I usually announce, "It's just me." Bill will respond, "No, it's especially you!" Small phrases like that keep my heart connected to his.

Ask a Question. Often we wait until those big nights out to engage in stimulating heart-to-heart conversation, but well-timed questions can keep us connected. Try some like these: "If you had one wish for us right now, what would it be?" or "If we could rendezvous anywhere on the globe right now, where would you like to go?" Find out what's in each other's hearts.

Drop a Hint. Tell your sweetheart, "While you're at work, think of last night." Place a special card or other romantic reminder in his or her briefcase or organizer. Call and leave a message on voice mail or e-mail that reminds your loved one of a special memory or a future date.

Tell a Joke. Humor and laughter brighten our day and draw us closer together. I look for funny comics and pithy quips that I can share out loud with Bill or slide under his door at work with a note.

Touch. Even if it's just a quick hug and kiss—or a five-minute one—touch provides much-needed emotional warmth in our high-tech world. Hold hands as you walk to an appointment. Link arms walking to the car. Every connection touches the heart.

Daydream. Take a few minutes to gaze at that well-worn photo of him you carry in your wallet. Walk through her side of the closet and touch her things. Pull out your photo album and reminisce as you look through the pages. Focus your thoughts and your love on your sweetheart.

Do Something Old-Fashioned. Swing by the florist shop and select a dozen perfect roses. Write a love note on stationery and send it by snail mail. Lovingly choose a chocolate treat for him or her at the grocery store.

Be Honest. Say "I miss you!" Sometimes couples argue just because their hearts long to be together. If you find yourself a bit edgy, ask yourself, "Could I be upset because I'm missing my sweetheart?" We need one another. It's perfectly okay to communicate that need. For example, I can say to Bill, "Honey, I miss you. I know you can't do anything about it right now, but I wanted you to know I was thinking about you." Let each other know that you care.

A good relationship
has a pattern
like a dance
and is built
on some
of the same
rules.

The partners
do not need
to hold on tightly,
because they move
confidently
in the same pattern,
intricate
but gay
and swift
and free,

like a country dance
of Mozart's. . . .
There is no place here
for the possessive clutch,
the clinging arm,
the heavy hand;
only the barest touch in passing.

Now arm in arm,
now face to face,
now back to back—
it does not matter which.
Because they know they are partners
moving to the same rhythm,
creating a pattern together,
and being invisibly nourished by it.

SOURCE UNKNOWN

Relax. When life is hectic, relax with exercise! Go for a walk, play a game together or take a swim. It's hard to be preoccupied when you are involved in an energetic activity. Our favorite escape is a quick dip in the ocean for some body-surfing. Get rid of stress together and return to life refreshed!

Pray. Hold each other and whisper your hopes, dreams, and desires.

Love sought is good,
but given unsought is better.

WILLIAM SHAKESPEARE